People never
forget two things,
their first love and
their first day in
New York City.

NEW YORK

CAPITAL OF FOOD

MURDOCH BOOKS
SYDNEY · LONDON

FOOD PHOTOGRAPHY
Lisa Nieschlag

NYC PHOTOGRAPHY
Julia Cawley

CONTENTS

NEW YORK – CAPITAL OF FOOD

MANHATTAN

4 Melting Pot

STORIES

5 Rooftop Bars

BROOKLYN

New York – Always a Good Idea

New York, one of the world's great cities, is a melting pot of cultures. Few other cities are as international and diverse as the Big Apple.

If you can make it here, you can make it everywhere! The city's many different cultures and nationalities are a mirror of the various waves of immigration throughout American history. And New York's culinary influences, ranging from hot Asian stir-fried noodles to spicy Mexican burritos and Jewish shakshuka, are just as multicultural and fascinating as its people.

New York – Capital of Food is the third cookbook that we dedicate to this melting pot on the Hudson River, this true treasure trove of delicious recipes, fabulous images and beautiful stories. We love this city and its diversity, which makes it a place like no other.

Do you know the Duke Ellington song *Take the A Train*? This jazz classic is a hymn to New York's oldest subway, line A, and we have taken it as our inspiration for exploring the city's multi-faceted culinary delights. Join us on our tour of discovery – this is the taste of New York!

Start your day with something sweet from one of the almost endless number of coffee shops. Take some time out for a picnic in the verdant oasis that is Central Park. Relax over a sumptuous dinner in one of the city's best restaurants, anywhere between the Upper West Side and Greenwich Village. And by all means stop to explore the lively neighbourhoods of Little Italy and Chinatown, setting yourself adrift in the hustle and bustle, exotic scents and special flair of these two unique pockets of New York. End your day with a bird's eye view of this incomparable city, perhaps over a cool Long Island Iced Tea in one of New York's trendy rooftop bars.

Join us on our trip to New York, the world's capital of food and culinary delights. The route is up to you.

Enjoy!

Lisa Nieschlag and Lars Wentrup

Lars Wentrup
Design

Lisa Nieschlag
Food photography

Julia Cawley
NYC photography

The Great Glander

Stevan Paul

The first thing Gustav acquired in New York was a daily routine. Giving his days structure made the foreign a little less foreign and provided something of a safety rope to which Gustav could cling while gingerly exploring his new life. It created a small piece of a self-determined world in the middle of this giant metropolis whose multitude of colours and deafening sounds was nothing if not sensory overload. Early in the mornings, while his room mates were still asleep, he would leave the student dorm where he had found an inexpensive room. The dorm was smelly; particularly in the mornings there seemed to be hardly any oxygen left in the corridors onto which the small rooms opened. The air smelt of second-hand clothes bins and leftover curry noodles from the Indian take-away on the corner. It smelt of stuffy socks, cold smoke and endless incense from the open kitchenette on the corridor. Outside the building, Gustav took a deep breath, zipped up his training jacket and started to run at a light pace. He enjoyed his early morning runs. He had worked out a route on foot and using a map and now ran the same round every morning. Running was the same as at home. It relaxed him as his steps on the asphalt turned into a monotonous rhythm that provided the perfect background for thinking. Within a few metres, he was already entirely in his own world, developing thoughts and ideas, while his body was busy running, and most of the time he came out of his runs a little wiser than when he started. He often thought of Katrin during his runs, of the life they had shared, of the small cinema that had first brought them even closer together and then driven them apart. He missed her. He had called her twice from the pay phone in the dorm. It had been very expensive, and there had been a lot of silences while he kept feeding coins into the phone until his palm was empty and the call was disconnected. Now he wrote to her regularly, asking how she was doing in her apprenticeship and whether life was good. He had not had any reply. In his letters, he also told her about New York and the art academy, but only sparsely and without exuberance. He never dropped a word about how difficult he found it to meet people; he had never been very good at talking, and having to speak English now almost sent him mute. Although he had done well in English at school, he was slow – too slow – to find the right words when talking to his room mates and other students, and so he often ended up thinking and smiling quietly while the people he was trying to talk to would give him a little wave, mutter *ahokaydoesntmatterseeya* and turn away, rolling their eyes. The lessons at

the art academy also dragged on slowly, without him contributing much to discussions. Earlier, professors and teaching staff had still encouraged him to speak, but then, over time, they had come to address the tall, silent German less and less often, favouring more dynamic exchanges during their classes, especially as he achieved good marks in his written papers and his practical work also suggested a talent for drawing and painting.

There was Sting singing the song about an *Englishman in New York* on the radio, and Gustav sang along quietly, *be yourself no matter what they say...* Sometimes his father would call the pay phone on the dorm corridor; he would sound excited, as if it was he who was in New York, delighted beyond words about his son, who was now living in a global metropolis. Each telephone conversation started by comparing the time of day here and there, and then father would want to know about everything, the sounds of the city, shops and businesses, the architecture and the cars in the streets, the food and the smells, the colours, the people: 'Come on, son, don't make me ask all the time, tell me more!' In the background, there would

be mother reminding them about the cost of long-distance calls to America. When father passed the telephone to her, she would usually start sobbing as soon as she heard Gustav's voice. 'The main thing is that you're happy!' she would cry again and again. Was he happy? Another good question ideal for pondering while running through this new city, with the definite answer always just ahead of Gustav Glander, always just out of reach. There was the *once-in-a-lifetime opportunity of this scholarship*, certainly, but there were also doubts and homesickness that accompanied him wherever he went. At least his regular runs gave him a little bit of a grounding. Twice every day, Gustav would tie the laces of his white runners with the three blue stripes and start running. 'It gets me to think differently,' he had told another student in the dorm by way of explanation, who in turn passed him a lit joint, uncomprehendingly. 'Try this; works just as well, dude!' he had said. But Gustav loved his

runs, especially the morning ones. For the first ten minutes he would run leisurely through Greenwich Village, where shutters were drawn up noisily as if the city was clearing its throat. Coffee was being brewed behind hesitantly opened windows; tea pots whistled energetically; and night owls were standing outside bakeries, biting hungrily into the first, oven-fresh croissants of the morning, chatting and laughing about their nights out, with smudged make-up and lightness on their faces.

After arriving at the Manhattan Waterfront Greenway, Gustav would stop briefly, each morning giving his full attention to the view and thinking of home. The similarity was astounding: There was the mighty Hudson River, steadily flowing in the morning sun, just like Lake Constance on the start to a beautiful spring day, and if Gustav just squinted a little, the skyscrapers on the other side would turn into a mountain range with one peak and ridge after another and police car sirens chirping in the valleys. There were mountain bikers overtaking runners, riding on their futuristic-looking bikes, mainly men in suits on their way to work, the legs of their business suits held together with clothes pins to keep them safely away from chain grease. Other men, slim, tall guys in sparkling tights and colourful shirts were roller-skating along the piers and past viewing platforms in elegant movements, like ballerinas, seemingly transfixed and fully focused, yet entirely aware of their visual impact at all times. In any event, the tourists holding their cameras excitedly

in their hands never had to wait long before one of these dancers on wheels would pass them by, in a theatrical choreography, their distant gaze laden with unknown meaning.

During one of his very first runs, just after he had moved into the student dorm, Gustav had stopped at *Tad's*, and this is how visiting this little deli became part of his daily ritual. *Tad's* was right on his way back to the dorm, only a block away. Of course, there was a coffee machine in the dorm, which dispensed a light brown fluid with an acidic aroma into paper cups for a few little coins. But Gustav was in no hurry to return to the dorm. At *Tad's*, there was a sweet smell of fresh bagels and roasted coffee beans, and there was the crackling sound of eggs being fried on the matte black metal cooker, above which the air shimmered. Everything was overlaid with the peppery aroma of warm sides of juicy pastrami sweating in the large smoker in the back yard. During the week, Gustav set aside a little money every day, doing without a second beer in the evenings, to save up for the house specialty on Saturdays: a glistening, deep red stack of wafer-thin, sliced, cured beef piled high between two slices of toast, still warm and juicy, fresh out of the oven, topped with – true indulgence! – flavourful, golden melted cheese that had nothing at all in common with the slices of processed cheese served at New York burger stands, but instead remotely reminded Gustav of the raw milk cheese from the mountain pastures of home. This was served with a sauerkraut salad with a slightly sweet, but still pleasantly acidic dressing. For a

few cents extra, one also got a pickled cucumber from one of the large preserving jars in the display, the cucumbers floating in the brine like green baby aliens.

'The usual?' asked the young chef across the room from behind the counter; he would have been about Gustav's age. Gustav raised his thumb approvingly and was served his breakfast only minutes later: toasted rye bread, two eggs, sunny side up, and a cup of coffee. It wasn't Saturday.

While he was eating, his eyes once again fell on the menu: *Tad's Deli – Jewish not kosher since 1950*. It was probably a typo; surely it should read *Ted's*. Gustav decided to ask as he returned his breakfast tray to the counter.Excuse me, I have a question.'
'Me too. Plenty of them!' said the chef without turning around. He skilfully cracked an egg and slid it out of its shell and onto the cooker with only one hand. 'What's your question?'
'Who's Ted?'
'Tad. It's Tad, and I'm Tad, my father is Tad and my grandfather was Tad and graced this beautiful country with his beautiful name. It's an abbreviation for Tadeusz, which Americans can't really pronounce, so you might suddenly find yourself being sued over a twisted tongue, that's why it's Tad. The only silly thing is that people now come to the counter, wanting to talk to Ted or pointing out a typo.' Tad slid a spatula underneath the sizzling eggs and transferred them gently onto a plate already holding some toast. He added a splash of ketchup to the plate from a plastic bottle, mumbling, 'I'll never get used to this,' and then turned around to the dining area, calling 'Two eggs, sunny side up, with, umm, yes, ketchup!' He looked at Gustav for the first time. 'You're not from here either, going by your accent.'
'I'm German.'
Tad grinned. 'That's okay.'
'And where are you from?'
'Greenwich Village, New York, sir! I'm American, born and bred into my grandfather's shop, into my father's shop. And I also had to be called Tad so we wouldn't have to print new menus. And unless I manage to run this shop down – and I'm working hard on it – my son will also have to be called Tad.' Tad laughed. 'Enough chatting, I have to get back to it.' He pointed his chin towards the dining area, where people had just sat down at two more tables. 'It's been a pleasure, umm...?'
'Gustav,' said Gustav.
'We all have our burden to carry,' said Tad, giving Gustav a little wave.
'See you tomorrow, big Gustav, and get your early extra egg, sunny side up!'★

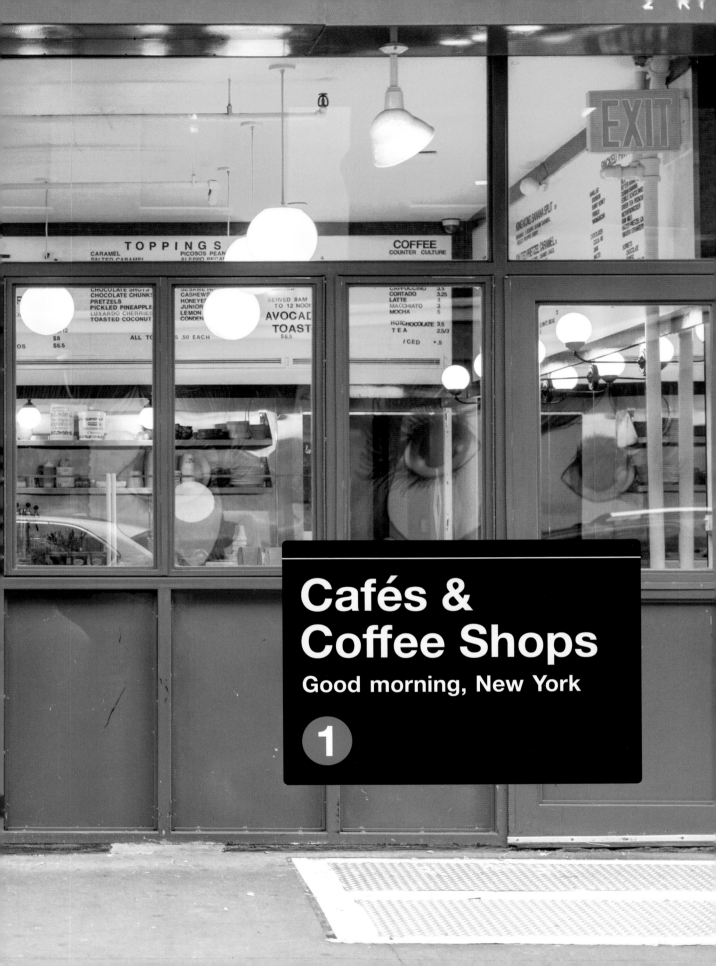

Cafés & Coffee Shops

Good morning, New York

1

Cashew caramel rolls

The origins of American sticky buns actually go back to Germany, where they are known as snails. In the US, these deliciously sweet pastries are often served for breakfast or as a dessert.

Ingredients

Makes 12 rolls

For the dough:
370 g (2½ cups) plain
  (all-purpose) flour
50 g (½ cup) blanched,
  ground almonds
2 tablespoons sugar
1–2 teaspoons vanilla extract
15 g (½ oz) fresh yeast
125 ml (½ cup) milk, lukewarm
60 g (¼ cup) butter
2 eggs, lightly beaten
Salt

For the filling:
50 g (¼ cup) brown sugar
1 teaspoon ground cinnamon
¼ teaspoon ground cardamom
50 g (scant ¼ cup) butter

For the sauce:
100 g (⅔ cup) salted, roasted
  cashew nuts
30 g (scant ¼ cup) chopped
  almonds
70 g (generous ¼ cup) butter
140 g (⅔ cup) brown sugar
50 ml (¼ cup) maple syrup

Also:
Butter for the tin
Flour for dusting

For the dough, combine the flour, almonds and both types of sugar in a mixing bowl and make a well in the centre. Crumble the yeast into the lukewarm milk and stir to dissolve. Pour the mixture into the well and gently stir to pull in a little flour from the sides. Cover with plastic wrap and leave to rise in a warm place for 20 minutes. Meanwhile, melt the butter in a small saucepan and leave to cool.

Add the cooled butter and whisked eggs to the yeast mixture together with 1–2 generous pinches of salt. Knead everything together for 5–7 minutes to make an elastic dough. Cover the bowl again and leave the dough to rise for 1½ hours.

Meanwhile, butter a 26 cm (11 inch) round tin. For the sauce, coarsely chop the cashew nuts and dry-roast the almonds in a pan until golden brown. Melt the butter in a saucepan, add the sugar and maple syrup and heat over low to medium heat, stirring well. Pour into the tin and sprinkle with cashews and toasted almonds.

For the filling, combine the sugar, cinnamon and cardamom. Melt the butter and leave to cool a little. Dust your worktop with flour and roll the proven dough out to a rectangle about 25 x 35 cm (10 x 14 inches) in size and 5 mm (¼ inch) thick. Brush with the melted butter and sprinkle with the cinnamon and cardamom sugar. Roll the dough up tightly, starting from the long side closest to you, and cut into 12 pieces about 2.5–3 cm (1–1¼ inches) wide. Place the pieces in the tin, cut side up, cover and leave to rise for another 20 minutes. Preheat the oven to 180°C (350°F).

Transfer the baking tray to the oven and bake the rolls until golden brown, about 25–30 minutes. Remove from the oven and immediately invert the tin onto a wire rack (make sure you place a sheet of baking paper underneath first). Leave the rolls to rest for 5 minutes, then remove the tin. Leave to cool and transfer the rolls onto a serving plate. Separate the rolls for serving.

Chocolate chip pecan blondies

Anybody who loves brownies will be delighted by these moist blondies! We have added white chocolate, milk chocolate and crunchy pecan nuts for extra deliciousness. If you do not have pecan nuts, simply substitute walnuts.

Lightly grease and then line a 21 x 26 cm (8 x 11 inch) baking tin with baking paper. Coarsely chop the pecan nuts. Heat the honey and sugar in a small pan. Add the nuts and toss for a few minutes to caramelise. Transfer to a sheet of baking paper, trying to keep the nuts as separate as possible.

Break the white chocolate into pieces. Melt over a double boiler with the butter, stirring occasionally. Be careful not to allow the boiler to get too hot. Don't worry if the butter separates on top of the melted chocolate. Leave to cool.

Preheat the oven to 180°C (350°F). Slice the vanilla pod open lengthwise and scrape out the seeds. Wash the lemon under hot water, pat dry and finely grate the zest. Combine the flour, salt and vanilla seeds. Add the eggs and sugar to a bowl and whisk for several minutes until thick and foamy. Stir in the cooled chocolate mixture and 2 tablespoons of the flour mixture. Fold in the remaining flour mixture to make a homogeneous batter. Do not overmix. Fold in the grated lemon zest, chocolate buttons or chips and pecan nuts with a spatula.

Spread the batter evenly in the tin and bake in the oven for 20–25 minutes. Use a skewer to test for doneness. If the top is getting too dark, loosely cover with aluminium foil. Take the tin out of the oven and leave to cool a little, before removing from the tin to cool completely.

Dust the blondies with icing sugar for serving.

Ingredients

Makes 12–16 small blondies

For the dough:
75 g (¾ cup) pecan nuts
1 tablespoon honey
1 tablespoon brown sugar
150 g (5½ oz) white chocolate
130 g (½ cup) butter
1 vanilla pod
1 small lemon
130 g (scant 1 cup) plain (all-purpose) flour
1 pinch salt
4 large eggs (about 70 g/ 2½ oz each)
75 g (⅓ cup) caster (superfine) sugar
50 g (⅓ cup) high-quality milk chocolate buttons or chips

Also:
Butter for the tin
Icing (confectioners') sugar for dusting

Strawberry lemon cookies

If you have no fresh strawberries available, these delicious summer cookies can be prepared with frozen fruit. If you are using frozen berries, add them without defrosting, otherwise they'll stain the cookie dough and make it too moist.

Ingredients

Makes 18–20 cookies

80 g (2¾ oz) white chocolate
80 g (½ cup) fresh strawberries
  (weight before cleaning/
  hulling)
225 g (1½ cups) plain
  (all-purpose) flour
1 teaspoon baking powder
1 pinch salt
125 g (½ cup) butter, softened
80 g (⅓ cup) sugar
1 large egg (about 70 g/2½ oz)
Zest of 1 small lemon, grated

<u>Also:</u>
Flour for shaping the cookies

Coarsely chop the chocolate. Clean, hull and finely dice the strawberries. Set aside to dry on kitchen paper.

Combine the flour, baking powder and salt in a bowl. Whisk the butter and sugar until creamy in a second bowl.
Stir in the egg and 1 tablespoon of the flour mixture, then gradually incorporate the remaining flour mixture to make a homogeneous dough. Carefully fold in the grated lemon zest, chocolate and strawberries with a spatula. Cover and chill the dough for 20 minutes.

Preheat the oven to 180°C (350°F) and line a baking tray with baking paper. Dust your hands with flour and shape the dough into balls of about 2.5 cm (1 inch) diameter. Add a little more flour if the dough seems too sticky. Arrange the balls on the baking tray, keeping them sufficiently apart, and gently press them to flatten. Bake the cookies in the preheated oven until golden brown, about 15–17 minutes, then transfer them to a wire rack and allow them to cool.

In the 1920s, the Waldorf Astoria Hotel in New York was famous for its signature **RED VELVET CAKE**. These days, red velvet cupcakes from the Magnolia Bakery in Greenwich Village are all the go. Whether cake or cupcake – this cookbook wouldn't be complete without a recipe!

Red velvet cheesecake

Preheat the oven to 150°C (300°F). Butter the tins and dust with flour. Ideally, also line the tin bases with baking paper.

Separate the eggs for the batter. Combine the buttermilk with the vinegar. Whisk the yolks with the sugar for 2–3 minutes, then stir in the buttermilk. Continue whisking for 8 minutes or until the mixture is thick and foamy. Melt the butter and leave to cool a little before stirring into the batter. Sieve the flour, beetroot powder, baking powder and salt on top and briefly whisk in. Beat the egg whites until stiff and gently fold in.

Divide the batter into two even portions (ideally weighing both portions to make sure you'll end up with two sponge bases of even size). Transfer each portion to a prepared springform tin. Put the springform tins into the oven, one after the other, and bake for 30–35 minutes. Use a skewer to test for doneness. Allow the sponges to cool a little before removing them from the tins. Transfer to a wire rack and leave to cool fully.

For the cookie crumble, increase the oven temperature to 170°C (325°F) and line a baking tray with baking paper. Place the biscuits inside a zip lock bag and pound them to a fine crumb with a rolling pin. Combine with the ground hazelnuts, sugar and salt in a mixing bowl. Melt the butter and add to the crumble mixture. Use your fingers to combine everything to a crumbly mass. Spread the mixture evenly onto the prepared baking tray and bake for about 8 minutes.

For the cheesecake cream, whisk the cream cheese, butter and vanilla extract in a bowl until smooth and creamy. Stir in the sieved icing sugar in several batches. Chill the cream for at least 20 minutes.

Place one sponge onto a cake platter with the domed upper side facing down. Spread with the cream. Top with the second sponge, flat bottom side down, and again spread with the cream. Spread the outside edges with the cheesecake cream and sprinkle all over with the cookie crumble.

Ingredients

Makes 2 springform tins (20 cm/8 inches)

For the dough:
4 large eggs (about 70 g/2½ oz each)
100 ml (generous ⅓ cup) buttermilk
1 teaspoon white wine vinegar
280 g (1¼ cups) caster (superfine) sugar
30 g (2 tablespoons) butter
170 g (scant 1¼ cups) plain (all-purpose) flour
30 g (1 oz) beetroot powder (from health food stores)
1 teaspoon baking powder
1 pinch salt

For the cookie crumble:
60 g (2¼ oz) wholemeal digestive biscuits (graham crackers)
20 g (scant ¼ cup) ground hazelnuts
1 tablespoon brown sugar
1 pinch sea salt
40 g (3 tablespoons) butter

For the cheesecake cream:
400 g (14 oz) double cream cheese, at room temperature
200 g (generous ¾ cup) butter, softened
½ teaspoon vanilla extract
150 g (1¼ cups) icing (confectioners') sugar, sieved

Also:
Butter and flour for the tins

Coffee smoothie

How about a coffee smoothie for breakfast instead of a hot cup of coffee? Frozen banana pieces make this smoothie deliciously cool and creamy – the perfect start for a hot summer day.

Peel and slice the bananas. Arrange the banana slices on a plate in a single layer and freeze for at least 45 minutes.

Meanwhile, dry-roast the flaked almonds in a pan until golden brown. Slice the vanilla pod open lengthwise and scrape out the seeds. Carefully open the tin of coconut milk without shaking it and remove 2–3 tablespoons of the firm coconut cream from the top. Whisk until smooth and set aside. Transfer 175 ml (¾ cup) coconut milk to a blender.

Add the chilled coffee, ground almonds, honey, cinnamon, frozen bananas and vanilla seeds to the coconut milk and blend everything to a creamy smoothie. Season with honey to taste. Divide the smoothie among two large glasses. Garnish with two dollops of coconut cream each and sprinkle with toasted almond flakes.

Ingredients

Makes 2 large smoothies

2 ripe bananas
1–2 tablespoons flaked almonds
½ vanilla pod
½ tin full-cream coconut milk
    (200 ml/generous ¾ cup)
250 ml (1 cup) strong, freshly
    brewed coffee, chilled
2 tablespoons blanched,
    ground almonds
2–3 tablespoons honey
½ teaspoon cinnamon

Blueberry & cream cronuts

Time magazine named cronuts, a trendy pastry creation by Dominique Ansel, among its '25 best inventions of 2013'. Adding a filling of airy whipped cream and a topping of blueberry frosting and crunchy pistachio sprinkle makes for a particularly fresh and summery take on this doughnut and croissant hybrid.

Ingredients

Makes 4–6 (depending on size)

About 500 g (1 lb 2 oz) puff
  pastry (frozen)
150 g (1 cup) fresh blueberries
  (alternatively frozen
  blueberries, defrosted)
About 150 g (1¼ cups) icing
  (confectioners') sugar
Zest of ½ small lemon
2–3 tablespoons pistachio
  kernels, chopped
150 ml (generous ½ cup) cream
1–2 teaspoons vanilla extract
1–2 tablespoons sugar
1 pinch ground cinnamon

Also:
Flour for dusting
About 1 litre (4 cups) neutral
  vegetable oil for deep-frying

Dust your worktop with a little flour. Place the puff pastry sheets next to each other, pushing them together with your fingers to seal the joints and create one long strip of pastry. Halve the pastry lengthwise and place one half on top of the other. Press firmly together. Repeat this process to end up with one thick strip of puff pastry. Roll out to about 1 cm (½ inch) thickness with a rolling pin. Use a large cookie cutter or glass to cut out 4–6 rounds, then use a 2 cm (¾ inch) cutter or shot glass to cut out circles from the centre of each round.

Heat the oil to about 175°C (350°F) in a deep fryer or saucepan. Dip the end of a wooden spoon or skewer into the oil. The oil is hot enough when bubbles rise immediately around the stick and the oil starts to sizzle. Carefully place two dough circles into the hot oil at a time and deep-fry over medium heat until golden brown, about 5 minutes per side. Don't let the cronuts get too dark! Remove the cooked cronuts from the oil with a slotted spoon. Shake off excess oil, drain on kitchen paper and leave to cool fully. Repeat with the remaining pastry.

Gently wash the blueberries and pat dry. Blend a third of the blueberries with a stick blender and pass through a fine sieve. Stir just enough icing sugar into the blueberry purée to make a thick, spreadable frosting. Whisk in the grated lemon zest.

Carefully halve the cronuts horizontally. Glaze the upper halves with the blueberry frosting, sprinkle with the chopped pistachios and set aside to firm up on a wire rack. Meanwhile, whisk the cream until stiff, gradually adding the vanilla sugar, sugar and cinnamon. Add more sugar to taste. Transfer the cream into a piping bag with a round nozzle.

Pipe the vanilla cream evenly onto the bottom cronut halves, sprinkle with the remaining blueberries and top with the iced cronut halves. These cronuts are best served immediately.

Double chocolate mud cake

This double chocolate mud cake is a must for any chocoholic. If you don't have fresh berries for garnish, dry-roast some mixed, chopped nuts and sprinkle the cake with these. If using nuts, garnish the cake before the ganache has fully set so that the nuts will stick to the cake.

Preheat the oven to 160°C (315°F). Butter the springform tin and dust with flour. Invert the tin and tap lightly to get rid of excess flour.

Break the chocolate into pieces. Melt over a double boiler together with the diced butter, stirring occasionally. Be careful not to allow the boiler to get too hot. Set aside to cool. Whisk the eggs, sugar and vanilla sugar until creamy, about 5 minutes, then gradually stir in the cooled chocolate and butter mixture.

Combine the flour, ground almonds or hazelnuts, cocoa powder, baking powder and salt. Stir the milk into the buttermilk, then gradually incorporate the dry and wet ingredients into the batter in several batches to make a homogeneous mixture. Be careful not to overmix though.

Spoon the chocolate batter into the prepared springform tin, smooth out the top and bake for about 70 minutes in the preheated oven. Use a skewer to test for doneness. The cake should still be a little moist inside. Remove from the oven and set aside to cool for 15 minutes. Transfer to a wire rack and leave to cool fully.

Break the chocolate for the ganache into pieces. Heat the cream in a saucepan. Remove from the heat just before it starts to boil. Add the chocolate pieces and stir to melt. Set the ganache aside to rest for about 30 minutes. It will thicken slightly as it cools. Whisk through once more and spread over the cooled cake. Leave the ganache to set and serve the cake garnished with fresh berries to taste.

Ingredients

**Makes 1 springform tin
(24 cm/9½ inches)**

240 g (8½ oz) high-quality dark
    (semi-sweet) chocolate
    (min. 60% cocoa)
290 g (scant 1¼ cups) butter
3 eggs
200 g (scant 1 cup) sugar
1–2 teaspoons vanilla extract
200 g (1⅓ cups) plain
    (all-purpose) flour
50 g (½ cup) ground almonds
    or hazelnuts
4 tablespoons cocoa powder
½ teaspoon baking powder
¼ teaspoon salt
150 ml (generous ½ cup)
    buttermilk
50 ml (¼ cup) milk

For the ganache:
140 g (5 oz) high-quality dark
    (semi-sweet) chocolate
    (min. 60% cocoa)
125 ml (½ cup) cream

Also:
Butter and flour for the tin
2 handfuls fresh raspberries or
    blackberries for garnish,
    to taste

Cookies & cream milkshake

Crunchy chocolate cookies with a creamy filling and a glass of cold milk are an amazing combination that will instantly make you forget any worries, and this milkshake works exactly the same magic! Top with extra chopped chocolate if you like.

Ingredients

**Makes 2 milkshakes
(about 250 ml/1 cup each)**

6 cream-filled chocolate cookies
    (e.g. Oreos), plus 2 more
    for garnish
4 scoops vanilla ice cream
300 ml (1¼ cups) full-cream milk
1–2 teaspoons cocoa powder
1 teaspoon vanilla extract

Also:
50 g (2 oz) dark (semi-sweet)
    chocolate

Melt the chocolate in a small bowl over a double boiler, stirring continuously. Set aside to cool slightly, then dip the rims of two glasses evenly into the melted chocolate. Allow excess chocolate to drip off and leave to cool.

Finely chop two chocolate cookies for garnish; coarsely chop the remaining cookies.

Add the ice cream, milk, coarsely chopped cookies, cocoa powder and vanilla extract to a blender and blend until smooth. Divide the milkshake among the two glasses, garnish with the chopped cookies and serve immediately.

Jewish espresso meringues

These Jewish espresso meringues are a fabulous hybrid between a dessert and an afternoon tea treat. Light and airy, these sweets are guaranteed to lift you out of any afternoon slump.

Preheat the oven to 100°C (200°F) and line a baking tray with baking paper. Whisk the egg whites and salt, gradually adding the baking powder and espresso powder. As the mixture starts to thicken, gradually add the two types of sugar, best spoonful by spoonful. Continue to whisk at high speed until the mixture forms glossy peaks.

Transfer the meringue mass to a piping bag with a star nozzle and pipe small rounds (4–5 cm/1½–2 inches) onto the baking paper, keeping them a little apart. Gently dry the meringues in the preheated oven for about 2 hours, trying not to open the oven door. Switch off the oven and keep the oven door just a tiny bit open with the end of a wooden spoon. Leave the meringues in the oven for another 10 minutes, then transfer them onto a wire rack and leave to cool fully.

Melt the chocolate over a double boiler; set aside and leave to cool a little. Meanwhile, dry-roast the almonds in a pan until golden brown. Dip the meringue tips into the melted chocolate, allow excess chocolate to drain and sprinkle with the chopped, toasted almonds. Leave to set.

Ingredients

Makes 30–40 small meringues

4 egg whites at room temperature (from large eggs)
¼ teaspoon salt
½ teaspoon cream of tartar powder
2 teaspoons instant espresso powder
175 g (generous ¾ cup) sugar
2–4 teaspoons vanilla extract
150 g (5½ oz) semi-sweet cooking chocolate
About 50 g (⅓ cup) chopped almonds

THE **BEAUTIFUL** AND **DAMNED**

F. Scott Fitzgerald

Crispness folded down upon New York a month later, bringing November and the three big football games and a great fluttering of furs along Fifth Avenue. It brought, also, a sense of tension to the city, and suppressed excitement. Every morning now there were invitations in Anthony's mail. Three dozen virtuous females of the first layer were proclaiming their fitness, if not their specific willingness, to bear children unto three dozen millionaires. Five dozen virtuous females of the second layer were proclaiming not only this fitness, but in addition a tremendous undaunted ambition toward the first three dozen young men, who were of course invited to each of the ninety-six parties—as were the young lady's group of family friends, acquaintances, college boys, and eager young outsiders. To continue, there was a third layer from the skirts of the city, from Newark and the Jersey suburbs up to bitter Connecticut and the ineligible sections of Long Island—and doubtless contiguous layers down to the city's shoes: Jewesses were coming out into a society of Jewish men and women, from Riverside to the Bronx, and looking forward to a rising young broker or jeweller and a kosher wedding; Irish girls were casting their eyes, with license at last to do so, upon a society of young Tammany politicians, pious undertakers, and grown-up choirboys.

And, naturally, the city caught the contagious air of entré—the working girls, poor ugly souls, wrapping soap in the factories and showing finery in the big stores, dreamed that perhaps in the spectacular excitement of this winter they might obtain for themselves the coveted male—as in a muddled carnival crowd an inefficient pickpocket may consider his chances increased. And the chimneys commenced to smoke and the subway's foulness was freshened. And the actresses came out in new plays and the publishers came out with new books and the Castles came out with new dances. And the railroads came out with new schedules containing new mistakes instead of the old ones that the commuters had grown used to....
The City was coming out! ★

Easy apple strudel

Many Germans emigrated to New York in the nineteenth century and they have left their culinary mark on the city, particularly in the form of various types of German pastries such as this easy apple strudel.

Ingredients

Makes 1 strudel

50 g (½ cup) walnuts
2–3 teaspoons honey
4 large apples
Juice of 1 small lemon
About 100 g (⅓ cup) butter plus
    2 tablespoons extra
100 g (½ cup) sugar
1 teaspoon cornflour
    (cornstarch)
1–2 teaspoons vanilla extract
1½ teaspoons ground cinnamon
2 heaped tablespoons ground
    hazelnuts
40 g (¼ cup) raisins (soaked in
    rum and drained, if preferred)
50 g (¾ cup) breadcrumbs
40 g (¼ cup) brown sugar
7 sheets fresh filo pastry
    (30 x 31 cm/12 x 12½ inches)

Also:
1 egg
2 tablespoons milk
Icing (confectioner's) sugar for
    dusting
Vanilla sauce or vanilla ice
    cream to taste, for serving

Preheat the oven to 190°C (375°F) and line a baking tray with baking paper.

Finely chop the walnuts. Dry-roast in a pan, add the honey and stir to caramelise. Remove from the pan and set aside to cool. Peel, core and quarter the apples and dice finely. Combine with half of the lemon juice. Heat 2 tablespoons butter in a frying pan. Add the diced apples and sugar and sweat over medium heat, then simmer for a few minutes. Stir in half of the lemon juice and simmer for a few more minutes. Whisk the cornflour into the remaining half of the lemon juice and add to the apple mixture. Continue to simmer the apples until soft over low heat, about 3 minutes. Combine with the vanilla sugar, cinnamon, hazelnuts, raisins and caramelised walnuts. Remove the pan from the heat.

Melt the remaining butter and leave to cool a little. Combine the breadcrumbs and brown sugar. Spread a tea towel on your worktop. Place one sheet of strudel pastry on the towel. Brush with melted butter and sprinkle with a little of the breadcrumb mixture. Top with another pastry sheet, again brush with melted butter and sprinkle with the breadcrumb mixture. Repeat until you have used up all of the pastry sheets. Spread the apple filling lengthwise across the bottom third of the top pastry sheet, leaving a 2.5 cm (1 inch) edge on the left and right. Fold the short pastry edges over the filling, then use the tea towel to roll up the strudel from the bottom, away from you. Transfer to the baking tray, seam side down.

Whisk the egg and milk and brush the strudel with the mixture. Bake in the preheated oven for about 25 minutes until golden brown. Remove from the oven and leave to cool for at least 15 minutes before serving. Dust generously with icing sugar, slice and serve warm. The strudel is best with vanilla sauce or vanilla ice cream.

Cherry rosemary pie

Grease the pie dish with butter and dust with flour. Invert the dish and tap lightly to get rid of excess flour. Combine the flour, cornflour, baking powder and salt in a mixing bowl. Add the chilled butter and rub in until the mixture resembles coarse breadcrumbs. Add the sugar. Whisk the egg yolks and water, add to the mixture and combine everything to a smooth dough. Set aside 225 g (8 oz) of the dough.

Dust your worktop with flour and roll out the remaining dough to a circle about 4 mm (¼ inch) thick. Line the pie dish with the dough. Press in well. Combine any offcuts with the 225 g (8 oz) of dough you have previously set aside. Cover with cling wrap and chill for about 30 minutes. Also refrigerate the pie pan with the dough lining.

Meanwhile, drain the cherries for the filling, reserving 100 ml (generous ⅓ cup) of the juice. Transfer the cherries and reserved juice to a saucepan together with the sugar and bring to a boil. Slice the vanilla pod open lengthwise and scrape out the seeds. Rinse the rosemary and shake dry. Add the vanilla seeds and pod and rosemary to the cherries and simmer for a few minutes. Wash the lemon under hot water and pat dry. Finely grate ½ teaspoon zest and juice the lemon. Whisk the cornflour into the lemon juice and add to the cherry mixture. Simmer everything for a few minutes until the mixture starts to thicken. Sweeten with honey to taste. Take the pan off the heat, remove the rosemary and vanilla and stir in the zest.

Preheat the oven to 175°C (350°F). Cover the dough in the pie dish with baking paper and some dried beans. Blind bake the base for about 15 minutes, then remove the baking paper and beans. Continue to bake for another 15 minutes. Leave to cool before topping with the cherry compote.

Dust your worktop with flour and roll out the remaining dough to a circle about 23 cm (9 inches) in diameter and 4 mm (¼ inch) thick. Cut out circles from the dough to allow steam to escape during baking. Place carefully onto the filling and seal the edges well, using a fork, to prevent the filling from leaking. Trim off any excess dough. Brush the dough with the remaining egg and sprinkle with sugar. Bake the pie in the preheated oven until golden brown, about 45–50 minutes. Cover with aluminium foil after about 25 minutes to prevent the top from getting too dark. Leave the pie to cool fully before removing it from the dish and cutting it, as the filling may be too runny otherwise. Dust with icing sugar to serve.

Ingredients

Makes 1 pie (20 cm/8 inch)
(use a pie dish or a tin with a loose base)

For the dough:
270 g (1¾ cups) plain
  (all-purpose) flour
35 g (generous ¼ cup) cornflour
  (cornstarch)
¼ teaspoon baking powder
1 generous pinch of salt
170 g (generous ⅔ cup) cold
  butter, diced
70 g (⅓ cup) sugar
2 egg yolks (from large eggs)
2 tablespoons cold water

For the filling:
About 680 g (1 lb 8 oz) pitted,
  sweetened morello cherries
  (370 g/13 oz drained weight)
50 g (¼ cup) sugar
1 vanilla pod
1 sprig rosemary
1 small lemon
2 tablespoons cornflour
  (cornstarch)
Honey to taste

Also:
Butter and flour for the tin
Flour for dusting the worktop
Dried beans for blind baking
1 egg, lightly beaten,
  for brushing
2 tablespoons brown sugar,
  for dusting
Icing (confectioners') sugar,
  for dusting

Central Park Picnic

Time out in a verdant oasis

②

Cauliflower bacon hand pies

The cauliflower for these delicious puff pastry pockets can, of course, also be steamed or boiled. However, it's well worth taking the time to roast it in the oven, as roasting really brings out the nutty caramel aroma that harmonises so well with bacon.

Ingredients

Makes 8 hand pies

1 small cauliflower
About 2 tablespoons olive oil
Sea salt
1 red onion
75 g (2½ oz) bacon
4 sprigs parsley
6–8 cherry tomatoes
50 g (¼ cup) crème fraîche
Salt, freshly ground pepper
Freshly grated nutmeg
275 g (9¾ oz) puff pastry
   (fresh or defrosted)
1 egg, whisked with
   1 tablespoon water

Preheat the oven to 200°C (400°F) and line a baking tray with baking paper. Trim and quarter the cauliflower. Brush each quarter with a little olive oil and sprinkle with sea salt. Transfer to the baking sheet and roast until golden brown, about 50 minutes. Turn after 25 minutes. If the cauliflower gets too dark, cover it loosely with aluminium foil. Test for doneness before removing from the oven; if the cauliflower is still firm, cover with foil, reduce the heat to 180°C (350°F) and cook for another few minutes. Leave the oven on.

Meanwhile, peel and finely dice the onion. Finely dice the bacon. Rinse the parsley, shake off excess water and coarsely chop the leaves. Quarter the cherry tomatoes and remove the stem bases.

Heat the olive oil in a frying pan. Add the onion and sweat for 5 minutes. Toss in the bacon and fry until crisp. Turn off the heat and stir in the quartered tomatoes and parsley.

Mash the roasted cauliflower with the crème fraîche, then stir in the bacon and tomato mixture. Season the mixture generously with salt, pepper and nutmeg.

Line the baking tray with fresh baking paper. Spread out the puff pastry sheets on a floured worktop and cut them into 16 even rectangles 6 x 9 cm (2½ x 3½ inches) in size. Transfer eight of the rectangles onto the baking sheet and brush the edges with a little whisked egg. Spoon 3–4 teaspoons of the filling onto each rectangle. Carefully stretch the remaining pastry rectangles and place them over the fillings. Use a fork to press the edges together firmly. Continue until all of the pastries are done. Brush the surfaces with the remaining whisked egg and bake the pies in the preheated oven (180°C/350°F) until golden brown, about 25 minutes.

Deli pasta salad

This delightful recipe with juicy cherry tomatoes, crisp pancetta and fresh zucchini hails from Little Italy and is very different from American pasta salads, which are typically made with mayonnaise, celery and apples.

Cook the farfalle pasta to al dente in boiling salted water according to the instructions on the packet. Drain, refresh under cold water and drain again thoroughly. Dry-roast the pine nuts in a pan until golden brown.

Wash and trim the zucchini, halve lengthwise and slice. Peel the shallot and slice into rings. Heat the olive oil in a frying pan and fry the zucchini and shallots for a few minutes. Remove and set aside. Dice the pancetta, add to the same pan and fry until crisp.

Remove the stem bases from the cherry tomatoes and halve or quarter the tomatoes. Deseed the capsicum, remove any white membrane and dice finely. Dice the sun-dried tomatoes, drain the olives and slice into rings. Rinse the basil, shake off excess water and pick off the leaves. Drain the bocconcini and cut or tear into small pieces. Combine all of the prepared ingredients in a large bowl.

Whisk all the ingredients for the dressing together, except the parmesan, and season with salt, pepper and sugar. Finely grate the parmesan and stir into the dressing. Toss the salad with the dressing. Leave to marinate for at least 2 hours before serving. Finally season again to taste with vinegar, oil, salt and pepper.

Ingredients

Serves 4–6

For the salad:
300 g (10½ oz) farfalle pasta
Salt
40 g (¼ cup) pine nuts
1 zucchini (courgette)
1 French shallot
Olive oil for frying
80 g (2¾ oz) pancetta
125 g (4½ oz) cherry tomatoes
1 yellow or orange
   capsicum (pepper)
80 g (½ cup) sun-dried tomatoes
   in oil (from a jar)
50 g (½ cup) pitted black olives
½ bunch basil
125 g (4½ oz) bocconcini

For the dressing:
4 tablespoons white balsamic
   vinegar plus extra, to taste
10 tablespoons olive oil
   plus extra, to taste
½ teaspoon dried oregano
½ teaspoon dried thyme
Salt, freshly ground pepper
Sugar
50 g (2 oz) parmesan

Fish burger

This burger is perfect for wrapping up in greaseproof paper for an al fresco picnic. Serve it together with home-made lemonade (page 65), a Greek lentil salad (page 71) and ham & cheese muffins (page 61) for an indulgent picnic in Central Park.

Ingredients

Makes 4 burgers

For the fish:
About 600 g (1 lb 5 oz) fresh
   salmon or redfish fillets
   (alternatively frozen fish
   fillets, defrosted)
Salt
Freshly squeezed lemon juice
50 g (⅓ cup) plain
   (all-purpose) flour
80 g (1⅓ cups) breadcrumbs
1 large egg (about 70 g/2½ oz)
2 tablespoons cream
4 tablespoons ghee

For the sauce:
2 large eggs (about 70 g/2½ oz
   each)
1 large bunch chives
8 tablespoons mayonnaise
2 splashes freshly squeezed
   lemon juice
Salt, freshly ground pepper

Also:
4 burger buns
Butter for spreading
4 cos lettuce leaves

For the sauce, hard-boil the eggs for about 9 minutes. Refresh under cold water, peel and chop finely. Rinse the chives, shake off excess water and slice finely. Combine the eggs and chives with the mayonnaise and season everything with some lemon juice, salt and pepper.

Gently rinse the fish fillets under cold water, pat dry and cut into eight even pieces. Season on both sides and drizzle with a little lemon juice. Transfer the flour and breadcrumbs onto two plates. Whisk the egg and cream until smooth in a third plate and season with salt. Turn the fish pieces first in the flour, then in the egg mixture. Allow excess egg to drain and then turn the fillets in the breadcrumbs.

Heat the ghee in a large frying pan over medium heat. Fry the fish pieces in batches until golden brown on both sides, about 5 minutes, turning them carefully so that the breading stays on.

Meanwhile, slice the bread rolls. Toast the cut sides and spread with butter. Wash and trim the lettuce leaves and tear into burger-sized pieces. Spread the bottom halves of the bread rolls with 2 tablespoon sauce each, then top with a lettuce leaf and two pieces of fried fish. Finally add the top halves.

Ham & cheese muffins

Muffins don't need to be sweet. This savoury version makes a great addition to any picnic. If you prefer vegetarian muffins, simply leave out the ham or increase the amount of corn and parmesan by 50 g (2 oz) each.

Preheat the oven to 180°C (350°F). Line a muffin tin with paper cases. Finely dice the ham and grate the parmesan. Wash, trim and finely slice the spring onions. Drain the corn well.

Whisk the eggs, crème fraîche and olive oil in a bowl until smooth. Combine the flour, baking powder, ½ teaspoon salt, a little pepper and the paprika powder. Stir into the egg mixture just enough to make a homogeneous batter. Do not overmix. Fold in the remaining ingredients with a spatula and divide the muffin batter among the paper cups using two tablespoons.

Transfer the tin to the preheated oven and bake the muffins for about 22–24 minutes until golden brown. Leave to cool inside the tin for 15 minutes. Remove and enjoy warm or cold.

Ingredients

Makes 12 muffins (one 12-hole muffin tin)

100 g (3½ oz) ham
100 g (3½ oz) parmesan
2 small spring onions (scallions)
150 g (5½ oz) corn (from a tin)
3 large eggs (about 70g/ 2½ oz each)
100 g (scant ½ cup) crème fraîche
100 ml (generous ⅓ cup) olive oil
200 g (1⅓ cups) plain (all-purpose) flour
1 teaspoon baking powder
Salt, freshly ground pepper
¼ teaspoon sweet paprika powder

Tuna pretzel bagel

Ingredients

Makes 8 bagels

For the dough:
450 g (3 cups) plain
   (all-purpose) flour
   plus some extra, if needed
50 g (⅓ cup) wholemeal flour
2 teaspoons salt
20 g (¾ oz) fresh yeast
1 teaspoon sugar
1 tablespoon canola oil

For the filling:
2 tins tuna in brine
   (150 g/5½ oz each)
1 yellow capsicum (pepper)
½ bunch chives
100 g (scant ½ cup) crème
   fraîche
150 g (⅔ cup) cream cheese
Salt, freshly ground pepper
1 pinch sugar
2 teaspoons freshly squeezed
   lemon juice
4 tomatoes
8 cos lettuce leaves

Also:
Flour for dusting the worktop
100 g (3½ oz) bicarbonate of
   soda (baking soda)
Sea salt or sesame seeds
   for sprinkling
Butter for spreading

Combine the two types of flour with the salt in a bowl. Crumble the yeast into 300 ml (1¼ cups) lukewarm water. Add the sugar and stir to dissolve. Add the yeast mixture and oil to the flour in the bowl. Knead everything together for about 6 minutes to make an elastic dough. Add a little more flour if the dough is too sticky. Cover the bowl with plastic wrap and leave the dough to rise in a warm spot for about 2 hours.

Knead the dough again on a lightly floured worktop and divide it into eight pieces of about 100 g (3½ oz) each. Make evenly thick sausage shapes out of the dough portions. Join the edges and press well to seal. There should be a hole about 4 cm (1½ inches) wide in the centre. Place the bagels onto a baking tray lined with baking paper. Cover and leave to prove for about another 30 minutes.

Preheat the oven to 190°C (375°F). Place a heatproof bowl of water on the bottom of the oven. The steam will prevent the bagels from getting too dry during baking and give them a beautiful crust. Stir the bicarbonate of soda into 1 litre (4 cups) water in a pot. Bring to a boil. Reduce the heat to a simmer. Place the bagels into the hot water, one at a time, and simmer for about 30 seconds each. Remove with a slotted spoon, drain and place them back onto the baking tray. Immediately sprinkle with sea salt or sesame. Bake the bagels in the preheated oven for 20–24 minutes, then leave to cool fully on a wire rack.

For the filling, drain and pull apart the tuna. Deseed the capsicum, remove any white membrane and dice finely. Rinse the chives, shake off excess water and slice finely. Combine the crème fraîche and cream cheese and stir in the remaining ingredients. Season the mixture with salt, pepper, sugar and lemon juice. Remove the stem bases from the tomatoes and slice. Wash and trim the lettuce leaves and tear into pieces. Next, halve the bagels. Toast the cut sides and spread with butter. Spread the bottom halves with the tuna cream and top with sliced tomatoes and lettuce. Top with the bagel tops.

Home-made lemonade

This home-made lemonade is the perfect refreshment on a hot summer's day. If you don't have any limes at hand, simply substitute lemons.

Set aside one large lime. Wash the remaining limes under hot water, pat dry and peel, making sure that the bitter white skin remains on the fruit. Squeeze the limes and reserve about 200 ml (generous ¾ cup) of the juice. Combine the lime juice, 50 ml (¼ cup) water, lime peel and sugar in a saucepan and simmer until the sugar has dissolved, stirring continuously. Strain the syrup through a fine-meshed sieve. Stir in 1–2 tablespoons honey to taste and leave to cool.

Rinse the mint, shake off excess water, pick off the leaves and divide them among the glasses. Add about 2 tablespoons of the cooled lime syrup to each glass. Wash the reserved lime under hot water, pat dry and cut into eight slices. Add 2–3 ice cubes and 1 slice lime to each glass and top with sparkling mineral water. Serve with straws.

Ingredients

Makes 8 small glasses

About 7 limes (depending
   on size)
100 g (½ cup) sugar
1–2 tablespoons honey
1 large bunch mint
16–24 ice cubes
1 litre (4 cups) sparkling
   mineral water, chilled

Hot dogs

Give your creativity free rein in concocting hot dog fillings – New York hot dogs are often served with sauerkraut, a tomato and onion sauce and plenty of Dijon mustard, but they are just as delicious with tomatoes, pickled cucumbers, grated cheese or a spicy chilli and mince meat sauce.

Ingredients

Serves 4 / makes 8 hot dogs

For the buns:
390 g (generous 2½ cups) plain flour
1 teaspoon salt
35 g (scant ¼ cup) sugar
12 g (½ oz) fresh yeast
175 ml (¾ cup) full-cream milk, lukewarm
2 tablespoons canola oil
1 egg

For the filling:
8 small hot dog sausages
½ small cucumber
4 tablespoons Dijon mustard
4 tablespoons ketchup
4 tablespoons mayonnaise
4 tablespoons fried onions

Also:
Flour for dusting the worktop and shaping the buns
1 egg yolk
2 teaspoons chives, chopped for garnish

For the hot dog buns, combine the flour, salt and sugar in a mixing bowl. Crumble the yeast into the lukewarm milk and stir to dissolve. Add the yeast mixture, oil and egg to the dry ingredients and process everything at low to medium speed to make a homogeneous dough (about 6 minutes). Cover the bowl with plastic wrap and leave the dough to rise in a warm spot for about 2½ hours.

Punch down the risen dough on a lightly floured worktop and divide it into eight even portions (about 85 g/3 oz each). Shape these first into rounds and then into oval buns. Add a little more flour if the dough seems too sticky. Transfer the buns to a baking tray lined with baking paper, cover and leave to prove for another 1 hour.

Preheat the oven to 190°C (375°F). Place a heatproof bowl of water on the bottom of the oven. The steam will prevent the buns from getting too dry during baking. Carefully cut shallow slits into the sides of the buns with a sharp knife to make sure their tops won't tear. Whisk the egg yolk until smooth with 3 tablespoons water and brush the buns thinly with the mixture. Transfer the baking tray to the preheated oven and bake the buns for about 18–22 minutes until golden brown. Set aside to cool on a wire rack.

For the filling, heat the hot dog sausages in hot, but not boiling water for about 5 minutes. Drain well. Wash the cucumber under hot water. Slice thinly. Halve the buns lengthwise, being careful not to cut all the way through. Spread both halves with mustard and lay sliced cucumber on the bases. Place the hot dogs inside and top with ketchup and mayonnaise. Garnish the hot dogs with fried onions and chives and serve immediately.

Greek lentil salad

If you feel like enjoying this delectable salad outdoors, simply transfer it to a screw-top jar. It's best to add the dressing to the jar first and then the tossed salad to keep everything fresh and crunchy.

Soak the lentils in cold water according to the instructions on the packet. Rinse and drain well. Wash and trim the lettuce and tear into bite-size pieces. Rinse the parsley, shake off excess water and coarsely chop the leaves. Peel the garlic and onion. Mince the garlic and slice the onion into rings. Dice the feta, halve the beetroots and also dice.

Transfer the lentils to a pot together with about 500 ml (2 cups) salted water or according to the instructions on the packet. Bring to a boil, reduce the heat to low and cook until al dente, about 25 minutes. Drain, refresh under cold water and drain again thoroughly.

Meanwhile, dry-roast the pine nuts in a pan until golden brown. Wipe out the pan with kitchen paper and reheat. Add the oil and sweat the onion and garlic over low to medium heat for 5–10 minutes. Combine the lettuce, parsley, pine nuts, cooled onion and garlic mixture, drained lentils, beetroot and feta in a bowl.

For the dressing, peel the garlic and crush with a garlic press. Stir the honey, cumin and cinnamon into the vinegar and whisk in the olive oil until thoroughly combined. Season the dressing generously with salt and pepper and gently fold into the lentil salad.

Ingredients

Serves 4

For the salad:
200 g (7 oz) Puy or French
   green lentils
1 small head oak leaf lettuce
   (alternatively lollo rosso)
1 small bunch parsley
2 small red onions
1 garlic clove
200 g (7 oz) feta
350 g (12 oz) cooked
   beetroot (beets)
Salt
40 g (¼ cup) pine nuts
1 tablespoon olive oil

For the dressing:
1 garlic clove
3 tablespoons red wine vinegar
1 tablespoon honey
¼ teaspoon ground cumin

¼ teaspoon ground cinnamon
6 tablespoons olive oil
Salt, freshly ground pepper

Spicy meatballs

Ingredients

Serves 4

For the meatballs:
500 g (1 lb 2 oz) mixed
   minced meat
1 small red onion
1 garlic clove
1 red chilli
2 eggs
50 g (¾ cup) breadcrumbs
Zest of 1 lime, grated
2 tablespoons freshly
   grated parmesan
Salt, freshly ground pepper
2 tablespoons olive oil

For the tomato sauce:
2 French shallots
1 garlic clove
1 tablespoon olive oil
1 tablespoon tomato paste
   (concentrated purée)
1 tablespoon balsamic vinegar
Sugar
400 g (14 oz) diced
   tomatoes (from a tin)
400 g (14 oz) tomato passata
   (puréed tomatoes)
Chilli flakes to taste
1 dash freshly squeezed
   lime juice
Salt, freshly ground pepper

Also:
Fresh oregano for garnish

To prepare the meatballs, place the minced meat into a mixing bowl. Peel and finely mince the garlic and onion. Wash and deseed the chilli and also chop finely. Combine the eggs, breadcrumbs, onion, garlic, chilli, lime zest and parmesan with the minced meat. Generously season the mixture with salt and pepper and knead well to combine. Use moistened hands to shape the mixture into small balls, then set the balls aside on a large, flat plate and refrigerate.

For the tomato sauce, peel the garlic and shallots. Mince the garlic and finely dice the shallots. Heat the olive oil in a large frying pan or wide saucepan. Add the shallots and garlic and sweat for a few minutes until translucent. Stir in the tomato paste and briefly fry. Deglaze with balsamic vinegar and add 1 teaspoon sugar. Stir everything for a few minutes to caramelise.

Add the diced tomatoes and passata and leave the sauce to simmer, uncovered, for about 30 minutes.

After about 20 minutes, heat the olive oil for frying the meatballs in another large frying pan. Fry the meatballs in two batches over medium to high heat until well browned all over. Season the simmering sauce with chilli flakes, lime juice, sugar, salt and pepper. Add the fried meatballs, cover with a lid and continue to cook for another 10 minutes over low heat. Season the sauce again with salt and pepper.

Remove the meatballs from the sauce and serve hot on a platter or with toothpicks as finger food or part of a buffet. Alternatively, leave to cool and pack as a snack on your next picnic. Serve the sauce as a dip on the side, garnished with fresh oregano.

Pastrami sandwich

If you ever visit New York, you definitely have to try a pastrami sandwich, where deliciously seasoned beef meets hearty sourdough bread. Some of the city's best pastrami sandwiches are said to be served at Katz's Delicatessen on the Lower Eastside.

For the sandwiches, preheat the oven to 75°C (150°F). Place the pastrami into a small roasting pan or baking dish with a lid. Pour in the stock. The meat should be covered with stock by about 2 cm (¾ inch). Cover the dish, place into the preheated oven and heat through for about 45 minutes.

Meanwhile, trim and very finely slice the cabbage for the coleslaw. Combine with ½ teaspoon salt in a bowl and massage well with your hands to soften the cabbage a little. Peel the carrot and cut into fine strips. This is best done using a julienne slicer. Peel and halve the shallot and slice into rings. Toss both with the cabbage. Whisk the mayonnaise, yoghurt, mustard and horseradish cream together. Season with lemon juice, salt, pepper and sugar, then combine with the coleslaw.

Whisk all the ingredients for the dressing together and season with pepper. Thinly slice the pickled cucumbers and toast the bread. Take the beef out of the oven, drain, transfer to a chopping board and slice as thinly as possible.

Spread the toasted bread with the dressing. Top half of the bread slices with coleslaw, plenty of pastrami and the sliced cucumbers. Place the remaining bread slices on top and press gently together. Halve the sandwiches and serve immediately.

Ingredients

Serves 4

For the sandwiches:
450 g (1 lb) pastrami, whole (available online, from deli butchers or fine food merchants, may need to be pre-ordered)
About 400 ml (1½ cups) beef stock
8 small pickled cucumbers
8 slices of sourdough bread

For the coleslaw:
200 g (7 oz) white cabbage
Salt
1 carrot
1 French shallot
5 tablespoons mayonnaise
2½ tablespoons yoghurt (3.5% fat)
1 teaspoon Dijon mustard
1 teaspoon horseradish cream
A little freshly squeezed lemon juice
Freshly ground pepper
Sugar

For the dressing:
6 tablespoons mayonnaise
2 tablespoons Dijon mustard
1 tablespoon honey
Freshly ground pepper

Onion bialys

Bialys are savoury pastries that are quite similar to bagels, but rather than a hole they have a hollow in the centre, which you can fill to your taste. The caramelised onions in this recipe are just one of many tasty options.

Ingredients

Makes about 8 bialys

For the dough:
400 g (2⅔ cups) plain
  (all-purpose) flour
1½ teaspoons salt
  (about 8 g/¼ oz)
8 g (¼ oz) fresh yeast
240 ml (1 cup) lukewarm water

For the filling:
1 large onion
1 garlic clove
1 tablespoon olive oil
1 teaspoon sugar
½ teaspoon sweet
  paprika powder
Salt, freshly ground pepper

Also:
Flour for dusting the worktop
Cream cheese for serving

To make the dough, combine the flour and salt in a bowl. Crumble the yeast into the lukewarm water and stir to dissolve. Add the yeasted water to the flour and combine everything, first for about 4 minutes at low speed, then for another 5 minutes at medium speed, to make an elastic dough. Cover the bowl with plastic wrap and leave the dough to rise for about 2 hours.

Divide the risen dough into eight even portions (about 75–80 g/ 2½–2¾ oz each). Shape these into round buns on a lightly floured worktop. Dust the buns with a little flour and transfer them onto a large tray. Cover again with plastic wrap and leave to prove for another 1½ hours.

For the filling, peel the garlic and onion. Mince the garlic and finely dice the onion. Heat the olive oil in a frying pan and sweat the onion and garlic for about 5 minutes. Add the sugar and continue to cook until lightly caramelised. Season the onion mixture with paprika powder, salt and pepper.

Preheat the oven to 240°C (475°F) and line a baking tray with baking paper. You may need two trays, depending on size. Use both thumbs to press hollows into the centres of the proven buns. Pick up the buns and turn them, holding them up and enlarging the hollow evenly until you have a thin bottom below a well of about 5 cm (2 inches) diameter with a lip about 2 cm (¾ inch) wide and high. Be careful to keep the bottom intact. Arrange the bialys on the baking tray, keeping them sufficiently apart. If necessary, divide them between two trays and bake one after the other.

Fill the bialys with the onion and garlic mixture and bake in the preheated oven until golden brown, about 12–15 minutes. Leave to cool and enjoy warm or cold with a spread of cream cheese.

Hash browns

In the US, hash browns are often only made of grated potatoes, salt and pepper, without egg or flour, but this causes them to fall apart very easily during frying. The potato mixture in this recipe holds together very well, and the hash browns turn out particularly crisp because the grated potatoes are rinsed and then squeezed out to remove excess starch.

For the hash browns, peel the potatoes and coarsely grate them. Transfer the grated potatoes to a bowl of water to rinse out their starch. This makes for particularly crisp hash browns after frying. Drain the potatoes into a strainer and then transfer them onto a clean tea towel. Twist the towel together to squeeze out as much liquid as possible. Return the grated potatoes to the bowl.

Peel and finely grate the carrot and onion. Add both to the potatoes, together with the egg and flour, and combine everything well. Season the mixture generously with sea salt, pepper or cayenne pepper and paprika powder.

Whisk all the ingredients for the dip together and season with salt and pepper.

Heat plenty of ghee in a frying pan over medium to high heat and fry the hash browns in batches of three. To do so, use two tablespoons to place small heaps of the potato mixture into the hot pan. Press flat and push together with the spoons. As soon as the hash browns have coloured nicely on the bottom, turn and fry the other side until golden brown as well. If they do not hold together well, stir a little more flour into the mixture. Drain on paper towel and serve immediately, sprinkled with sea salt. Serve with the dip. These hash browns taste great hot or cold.

Ingredients

Serves 4

For the hash browns:
1 kg (2 lb 4 oz) waxy potatoes
1 carrot
1 small onion
1 egg
About 3 tablespoons plain
 (all-purpose) flour
Sea salt, freshly ground pepper
 or cayenne pepper
Sweet paprika powder

For the sour cream dip:
200 g (generous ¾ cup)
 sour cream
1 tablespoon yoghurt
1 tablespoon chives, chopped
1 splash of freshly squeezed
 lemon juice
Salt, freshly ground pepper

Also:
Plenty of ghee for frying

81

Capital of Food

The perfect dinner

3

Caesar salad

According to the original New Yorker recipe by Cesare Gardini, caesar salad is only served with croutons and parmesan. We have added a garnish of delicate chicken breast strips. However, you can also top your caesar salad with avocado, prawns or fresh tomatoes if you prefer.

Ingredients

Serves 4

For the salad:
2 chicken breast fillets
2 large slices of light
   sourdough bread
2 cos lettuce hearts
3 tablespoons canola oil
Salt, freshly ground pepper
1 tablespoon butter

For the dressing:
30 g (1 oz) parmesan
1 garlic clove
1–2 anchovies in oil,
   to taste
1 egg yolk
½ teaspoon Dijon mustard
2 teaspoons white wine vinegar
Sea salt
100 ml (generous ⅓ cup)
   canola oil
2 tablespoons olive oil
Juice of ½ lemon
2–3 tablespoons buttermilk

Also:
Shaved parmesan
   for garnish

For the dressing, grate the parmesan finely. Peel the garlic and crush with a garlic press. Finely mince the anchovies. Combine the egg yolk, mustard, vinegar and 1 pinch of sea salt in a clean bowl. Measure the canola and olive oil in a measuring cup. Stand the bowl on a damp tea towel to ensure that it won't slip. Whisk the ingredients in the bowl using the whisk attachment of an electric mixer. Start by adding the oil in drops to prevent the mixture from separating.

Once the mayonnaise has thickened a little, add the oil in a thin, steady stream. Continue to whisk until all of the oil has been added to the bowl and the mayonnaise has a thick, creamy consistency. Stir in the grated parmesan, garlic, anchovies, lemon juice and buttermilk and season the dressing with sea salt.

For the salad, take the chicken breast fillets out of the fridge. Cut the bread into small dice. Wash and trim the cos lettuce and tear into bite-size pieces. Heat 2 tablespoons oil in a large pan. Salt the chicken breast, add to the pan and fry until golden brown on both sides, about 5–6 minutes, depending on thickness. Season with pepper. Transfer the meat onto a chopping board, cover with aluminium foil and leave to rest for 5–10 minutes. Wipe the pan, add the remaining oil and heat together with the butter. Fry the diced bread until crisp, stirring frequently. Season with salt and pepper.

Toss the lettuce with three quarters of the dressing and the croutons and divide the salad among four plates. Slice the chicken breast and arrange on top. Drizzle with the remaining dressing and serve garnished with shaved parmesan.

Corn chowder

This soup recipe is a nod to New England clam chowder, a true classic of American cooking made from succulent clams, as the name suggests. In this recipe, hearty pancetta meets sweet corn in a combination that is just as rich in flavour as the original.

For the soup, peel and finely dice the onion. Wash and trim the celery and also dice finely. Heat the butter and olive oil in a saucepan. Add the onion and celery and sweat for 5–10 minutes before adding the corn, reserving 2 tablespoons for garnish. Continue to sauté briefly. Deglaze with white wine and simmer until the liquid has evaporated. Add just enough stock to cover the vegetables and simmer the soup for about 15 minutes.

Meanwhile, finely dice the pancetta. Peel and dice the potatoes. Wash and trim the spring onions and slice into rings. Heat the oil in a frying pan and fry the pancetta until crisp. Add the diced potatoes and fry until gently browned all over. Stir in the spring onions, season everything with pepper and take the pan off the heat.

Whisk the cream into the soup and blend everything until smooth using a stick blender. Add more stock if the soup is too thick. Finally pass the soup through a fine sieve and return to the saucepan. Heat up again and stir in the reserved corn. Season everything with lemon juice, marjoram, thyme, salt and pepper. Divide among soup plates and serve garnished with the pancetta, diced potatoes and spring onions.

Ingredients

Serves 4 (as a main)

For the soup:
1 small onion
1 large stick celery
1 tablespoon butter
1 tablespoon olive oil
600 g (1 lb 5 oz) corn (from a tin)
75 ml (⅓ cup) white wine
About 500 ml (2 cups) vegetable
  stock
100 ml (generous ⅓ cup) cream
1–2 teaspoons freshly squeezed
  lemon juice
1 teaspoon dried marjoram
1 teaspoon dried thyme
Salt, freshly ground pepper

For the garnish:
6 slices of pancetta
2–3 potatoes, boiled in
  their skins
2 small spring onions (scallions)
1 tablespoon olive oil

Sweet potato & kale frittata

This delicious frittata is very versatile and makes a lovely centrepiece for lunch or a perfect light supper. If you cannot get fresh kale, simply substitute frozen kale or English spinach.

Ingredients

Serves 4 / makes 1 round baking dish (26 cm/10½ inches)

1 large sweet potato
   (about 450–500 g/
   14 oz–1 lb 2 oz unpeeled)
1 red onion
3 tablespoons olive oil
Salt, freshly ground pepper
120 g (4¼ oz) kale
2 sprigs thyme
6 eggs
150 ml (generous ½ cup) cream
75 ml (⅓ cup) milk
75 g (2½ oz) goat's curd
1 generous pinch of freshly
   grated nutmeg
¼ teaspoon chilli flakes
75 g (2½ oz) soft goat's cheese

Preheat the oven to 210°C (410°F). Peel the sweet potato and cut into dice 2 cm (¾ inch) in size. Peel and halve the onion and cut into thin wedges. Transfer both to a baking dish and toss with the olive oil. Season with salt and pepper. Cook in the preheated oven for about 15 minutes, turning once.

Meanwhile, wash and trim the kale. Remove the thick ribs and tear into bite-size pieces. Bring salted water to a boil in a saucepan. Add the kale and blanch for 2 minutes. Drain, refresh under cold water and spin dry in a salad spinner. Rinse the thyme, shake off excess water and pick off the leaves.

Whisk the eggs with the cream, milk, goat's curd and thyme. Season with pepper, nutmeg and chilli. Dice the soft goat's cheese or crumble with your fingers.

Take the baking dish out of the oven and toss the kale well with the diced sweet potato and onion wedges. Pour the egg mixture over the vegetables and sprinkle with the crumbled or diced goat's cheese. Return the dish to the oven and bake until nicely browned on top, about 20–25 minutes. If you would like a bit more colour, switch the oven to grill for the last few minutes of cooking. Slice the frittata to serve.

Chicken à la king

To make the chicken stock, put the chicken in a large saucepan. Wash, trim and coarsely dice the carrots, celery and leek. Peel the garlic and onion and halve or quarter. Rinse the herbs. Add to the chicken together with 2 teaspoons salt and the peppercorns. Cover everything with water and bring to a boil over medium heat. Cover and simmer for about 1½ hours. Take the saucepan off the heat. Leave the chicken to cool in the stock and then transfer to a chopping board. Pass the stock through a sieve and season with salt. Set aside about 400 ml (1½ cups) for the chicken à la king (the rest can be easily frozen for later use). Skin and debone the chicken and cut into bite-size pieces. Set aside.

Peel and finely dice the onion for the chicken à la king. Deseed the capsicum, remove any white membrane and dice finely. Wipe the mushrooms with paper towels, trim and cut into quarters or eighths. Blanch the peas in boiling salted water for a few minutes. Strain and refresh under cold water. Wash the lemon under hot water and pat dry. Finely grate 2 teaspoons zest and juice the lemon.

Heat 1 tablespoon oil in a frying pan. Add the onion and capsicum and sweat for about 10 minutes until the vegetables are done, but are still firm to the bite. Remove and set aside. Heat the remaining oil in the same pan and fry the mushrooms for about 5 minutes. Season with salt and pepper and add to the capsicum.

Melt the butter in a large saucepan over low to medium heat. Dust with the flour and sweat briefly, being careful not to allow the flour to take on any colour. Slowly stir in the stock, milk and cream and simmer until the mixture thickens. Continue stirring to prevent clumps from forming. Season the sauce with salt and pepper. Add the meat and vegetables and simmer everything for a few minutes. Whisk in a little more stock or milk if the sauce is too thick. Stir in the lemon juice and zest and continue to simmer the chicken à la king for another 5–10 minutes. Season with salt, pepper, nutmeg and paprika powder and serve with toasted white bread or rice.

Ingredients

Serves 4

For the chicken stock:
1 chicken for boiling
   (about 1.5 kg/3 lb 5 oz)
3 carrots
1 large stick celery
1 leek
2 garlic cloves
1 onion
1 sprig rosemary
3 sprigs thyme
Salt
1 teaspoon black peppercorns

For the chicken à la king:
1 red onion
1 red capsicum (pepper)
1 yellow capsicum (pepper)
200 g (7 oz) button mushrooms
150 g (5½ oz) frozen peas
Salt
1 lemon
2 tablespoons olive oil
Freshly ground pepper
5 tablespoons butter
5 tablespoons plain
   (all-purpose) flour
About 400 ml (1½ cups) chicken
   stock (see above)
About 150 ml (generous ½ cup)
   milk
150 ml (generous ½ cup) cream
Freshly grated nutmeg
Sweet paprika powder

Also:
Toasted white bread or cooked
   long-grain rice, for serving

Seafood gumbo

The word *gumbo* is derived from the Angolan word *kingombo* and simply means okra. And this is no coincidence, as these green pods are the main ingredient in this Creole seafood stew. They also give it its creamy consistency.

Ingredients

Serves 4–6

3 garlic cloves
2 onions
1 red capsicum (pepper)
1 yellow capsicum (pepper)
3 sticks celery
250 g (9 oz) small okra pods
1 red chilli
100 ml (generous ⅓ cup)
  canola oil
100 g (⅔ cup) plain
  (all-purpose) flour
1 teaspoon smoked
  paprika powder
1 teaspoon chilli flakes
1 teaspoon dried oregano
½ teaspoon dried thyme
½ teaspoon dried rosemary
About 800 ml (3¼ cups) fish
  stock (or vegetable stock)
600 g (1 lb 5 oz) peeled
  tomatoes (from a tin)
Salt, freshly ground pepper
Cayenne pepper
Sugar
600 g (1 lb 5 oz) fresh prawns
  (shrimp), peeled and deveined
  (or frozen prawns, defrosted)

Also:
3 spring onions (scallions)
Parsley

Peel the garlic and onion. Mince the garlic and dice the onion. Wash and trim the capsicum and celery. Cut into small strips or slice finely. Trim the stems and dry tips off the okra pods. Cut into bite-size pieces. Wash the chilli. Remove the stem, halve, deseed and chop finely.

Heat the oil in a saucepan with a thick base over medium heat. Dust with the flour and sweat until browned, stirring continuously. This can take up to 15 minutes. As soon as this roux has browned lightly, add the prepared ingredients and sweat everything for about 5 minutes.

Stir in the spices and dried herbs and fry briefly before deglazing with 250 ml (1 cup) fish stock. Simmer to reduce. Meanwhile, remove the stem bases from the tomatoes and chop coarsely. Add the tomatoes to the stew and bring everything to a boil. Season with salt and pepper and continue to simmer for about 20–30 minutes, gradually adding and incorporating the fish stock until the gumbo is rich and creamy. Season again with salt, pepper, cayenne pepper and sugar.

Stir in the prawns for the last 4 minutes of cooking. Wash, trim and finely slice the spring onions. Rinse the parsley, shake off excess water and pick off the leaves. Divide the gumbo among plates and serve garnished with sliced spring onions and parsley.

Red cabbage slaw

Served with a T-bone steak and potato wedges (page 102), this crunchy red cabbage salad with carrots and walnuts makes for a wonderful dinner. Alternatively, you can transfer it to a screw-top jar to take to the office and enjoy for lunch.

For the salad, remove the outer leaves from the cabbage and trim off any discoloured sections. Cut out the core in a wedge shape and finely slice the cabbage. Transfer to a large bowl, sprinkle with 1–2 teaspoons salt and leave to sit for a little, then massage well with your hands to soften the cabbage. We recommend wearing kitchen gloves for doing this.

Peel the carrots and cut into fine strips using a julienne slicer. Peel and halve the onion and cut into thin rings. Heat the oil in a frying pan. Add the onion and sweat for 5 minutes. Add to the red cabbage and carrots and toss everything to combine.

Whisk all the ingredients for the dressing together and season with salt and pepper. Combine the dressing with the salad. Refrigerate the red cabbage slaw for at least 1 hour to allow the flavours to marry.

Coarsely chop the walnuts and dry-roast in a frying pan until they smell fragrant. Add the honey and toss with the nuts for a few minutes to caramelise. Rinse the chives, shake off excess water and slice finely. Leave the nuts to cool, then sprinkle over the salad as garnish together with the chives.

Ingredients

Serves 4

For the salad:
½ head red cabbage
   (about 700 g/1 lb 9 oz)
Salt
2 small carrots
1 onion
1 tablespoon canola oil

For the dressing:
150 g (generous ½ cup) yoghurt
3 tablespoons mayonnaise
1 teaspoon Dijon mustard
2 tablespoons white wine
   vinegar
1 teaspoon sugar
Salt, freshly ground pepper

Also:
75 g (½ cup) walnuts
1 tablespoon honey
4 chives

T-bone steak with potato wedges

Steak with potato wedges and BBQ sauce – now that's true soul food. If you prefer a lighter, fresher meal, pair the T-bone steaks with a big green salad and top everything with pine nuts.

Ingredients

Serves 4 (with healthy appetite)

For the steaks:
4 small dry-aged T-bone steaks
   (500 g/1 lb 2 oz each)
Sea salt
Canola oil for frying
Freshly ground black pepper

For the potato wedges:
1 kg (2 lb 4 oz) evenly
   sized waxy potatoes
1 sprig rosemary
2 sprigs thyme
2–3 tablespoons olive oil
1 teaspoon sea salt
1 teaspoon sweet
   paprika powder
1 pinch garlic powder
1 pinch chilli powder

Also:
BBQ sauce, to taste, for serving
   (home-made, page 105)

For the steaks, take the meat out of the refrigerator and leave to rest at room temperature for at least 1 hour before frying.

For the potato wedges, preheat the oven to 180°C (350°F) fan-forced (alternatively 200°C/400°F in a standard oven) and line a baking tray with baking paper. Brush the potatoes well, wash and pat dry thoroughly, then cut into quarters or eighths lengthwise, depending on size. Make the wedges as evenly thick as possible. Rinse the rosemary and thyme and shake off excess water. Pick off the leaves and finely chop.

Combine the olive oil with the sea salt and paprika, garlic and chilli powders in a large bowl. Stir in the chopped leaves. Add the potato wedges and toss to coat evenly. Transfer the potato wedges onto the baking tray in a single layer and bake until golden brown and cooked through, about 20–30 minutes depending on size. If you would like a bit more colour, switch the oven to the grill (broiler) function for the last few minutes of cooking. Reduce the oven temperature to 110°C (225°F).

Carefully pat the steaks dry and sprinkle with sea salt on both sides. Heat two frying pans at the same time, if possible, and add 1–2 tablespoons canola oil to each pan to heat. Add the steaks and sear for 1½–2 minutes per side over medium to high heat until browned well. Use kitchen tongs for turning.

Season the steaks with pepper on both sides, transfer to the roasting rack in the oven and continue to cook for another 12–17 minutes, depending on thickness. Ideally check the core temperature with a food thermometer. For medium steaks, the centre should have about 55–58°C (131–136°F). Transfer the steaks onto a chopping board, cover loosely with aluminium foil and leave to rest briefly. Cut the steaks into slices or serve whole if you prefer. Serve with the potato wedges and BBQ sauce.

BBQ sauce

BBQ sauce is an American classic and no New York cookbook worth its salt should be without a recipe for it. This sauce is reduced slowly over low heat to get a thick, syrup-like consistency. Its rich combination of flavours and aromatic spices make it the perfect accompaniment to various meat and BBQ dishes.

Peel the garlic and onion. Mince the garlic and dice the onion. Drain the peeled tomatoes, reserving the juice, and dice coarsely. Deseed the capsicum, remove any white membrane and slice into strips. Wash the chilli. Remove the stem, deseed and chop finely. Dice the apricots.

Heat the oil in a saucepan. Add the onions and garlic and sweat for a few minutes. Stir in the sugar and continue to cook until caramelised. Deglaze with cola, vinegar, Worcestershire sauce and orange juice. Bring everything to a boil and simmer, uncovered, for about 20 minutes over medium heat to reduce.

Add the diced tomatoes, reserved juice, capsicum, chilli, apricots, ½ teaspoon salt, star anise and cinnamon and return to a boil. Reduce the heat to low and simmer for about 1 hour, then strain through a fine sieve, squeezing out all liquid from the vegetables. Season the sauce with salt, pepper, chilli flakes and Worcestershire sauce. If it is still too thin, return the sauce to the saucepan and simmer again over a low heat until it has the desired consistency.

Fill the BBQ sauce into a small, clean screw-top jar or sterilised bottles. Leave to cool fully and then seal. The sauce will keep for about 2 weeks in the refrigerator.

Ingredients

Makes about 500 ml (2 cups)

2 garlic cloves
2 large red onions
800 g (1 lb 12 oz) peeled tomatoes (from a tin)
1 red capsicum (pepper)
1 red chilli
50 g (¼ cup) dried apricots
2 tablespoons canola oil
100 g (½ cup) brown sugar
150 ml (generous ½ cup) cola
100 ml (generous ⅓ cup) red wine vinegar
1½ tablespoons Worcestershire sauce, plus a little extra for seasoning
Juice of ½ orange
Salt
1 star anise
½ cinnamon stick
Freshly ground pepper
Chilli flakes

New York style pizza

To make the dough, combine the flour and sugar in a bowl. Make a well in the centre. Crumble the yeast into the lukewarm water and stir to dissolve. Pour the yeast mixture into the well and gently stir in a little flour from the edges. Cover the bowl with plastic wrap and leave until the yeast mixture develops bubbles, about 20 minutes.

Add the olive oil and salt to the dough and knead everything strongly for at least 5 minutes. Cover the bowl again and leave the dough to rise for 1½ hours.

For the sauce, peel the garlic and shallots. Mince the garlic and finely dice the shallots. Rinse the thyme and rosemary and shake dry. Heat the olive oil in a saucepan over medium heat. Add the shallots and garlic and sweat for a few minutes until translucent. Deglaze with the red wine and simmer to reduce until most of the liquid has evaporated. Stir in the diced tomatoes and passata, add the thyme, rosemary and bay leaf and bring everything to a boil. Simmer the sauce, uncovered, over low to medium heat for about 45 minutes until it has a rich, creamy consistency. Season to taste with balsamic vinegar, oregano, chilli powder, salt, pepper and sugar. Remove the sprigs of thyme and rosemary and the bay leaf.

Preheat the oven to 200°C (400°F) fan-forced (220°C/425°F in a standard oven) and line a baking tray with baking paper. Dust your worktop with flour and roll out the dough thinly to the size of your baking tray. Fold back the edges to make them double the thickness of the remaining dough. Transfer the dough to the baking sheet and prick it all over with a fork (except the edges), then sprinkle with a thin layer of mozzarella all over (including the edges). Distribute the sauce evenly across the pizza, leaving out the edges. Top the pizza with salami and capers to taste. Sprinkle with the remaining mozzarella. Bake the pizza on the bottom rack until crisp. This should take 15–20 minutes in a fan-forced oven and a bit longer in a standard oven. (If you have a pizza stone, bake the pizza on the stone to make it extra crisp.)

Rinse the basil, shake off excess water and tear the leaves into smaller pieces. Take the pizza out of the oven, cut into slices and serve garnished with basil.

Ingredients

Makes 1 tray

For the base:
280 g (scant 2 cups) plain (all-purpose) flour, plus some extra for dusting
½ teaspoon sugar
15 g (½ oz) fresh yeast
150 ml (generous ½ cup) lukewarm water
2 tablespoons olive oil
½ teaspoon salt

For the sauce:
1 garlic clove
2 French shallots
3 sprigs thyme
1 sprig rosemary
1 tablespoon olive oil
75 ml (⅓ cup) dry red wine
400 g (14 oz) diced tomatoes (from a tin)
250 g (9 oz) tomato passata (puréed tomatoes)
1 bay leaf
1 tablespoon balsamic vinegar
1 teaspoon dried oregano
1 pinch chilli powder, to taste
Salt
Freshly ground pepper
Sugar

For the topping:
About 200 g (1½ cups) grated mozzarella
About 80 g (2¾ oz) fennel salami, sliced thinly
Capers, drained, to taste
2 sprigs basil

109

Veggie jambalaya

**Jambalaya comes from the Cajun cuisine of the southern states of the US.
This stew is traditionally made with rice, vegetables, chicken, seafood and chilli.
We have opted for a vegetarian version that still celebrates the *holy trinity* of
jambalaya: onions, mild green capsicum and celery.**

Peel and finely dice the carrots and onion and mince the garlic.
Wash and trim the celery. Halve lengthwise and slice into thin
half moon shapes. Deseed the capsicum, remove any white
membrane and slice into bite-size strips. Wash and trim the
zucchini, halve lengthwise and slice.

Heat the oil in a saucepan with a thick base. Add the onions and
garlic and sweat for a few minutes until translucent. Stir in the
carrots, celery and capsicum and fry briefly. Add the spices and
dried herbs and fry briefly before deglazing with vegetable stock.
Bring everything to a boil. Meanwhile, remove the stem bases
from the peeled tomatoes and dice the tomatoes coarsely. Rinse
and drain the kidney beans. Add the beans and tomatoes to the
saucepan and season everything well with salt, pepper, cayenne
pepper and sugar.

Simmer the vegetables for about 5 minutes, then add the sliced
zucchini and rice. Continue to simmer over low to medium heat
for about 20 minutes, stirring frequently, until the rice is cooked
al dente. Remove the bay leaf.

Meanwhile, rinse the parsley, shake off excess water and coarsely
chop the leaves. Divide the jambalaya among plates and serve
garnished with parsley.

Ingredients

Serves 4

2 carrots
1 large onion
2 garlic cloves
2 sticks celery
1 green capsicum (pepper)
1 red capsicum (pepper)
1 yellow capsicum (pepper)
1 zucchini (courgette)
3 tablespoons canola oil
1½ teaspoons smoked
   paprika powder
½ teaspoon dried thyme
½ teaspoon dried oregano
1 bay leaf
800 ml (3¼ cups) vegetable
   stock
800 g (1 lb 12 oz) peeled
   tomatoes (from a tin)
100 g (3½ oz) kidney beans
Salt, freshly ground pepper
Cayenne pepper
Sugar
200 g (1 cup) long-grain rice
½ bunch parsley

22 AUGUST 1967

Uwe Johnson

On weekdays, Gesine Cresspahl buys her copy of the *New York Times* from the newsstand, because the delivery boy might be too late. On the subway platform, she folds her paper across and again lengthwise so she can hold on to it amidst the crowd pushing through the doors and even read the first page of the eight-column broadsheet from top to bottom, squeezed tightly between elbows and shoulders, in the fifteen minutes for which the subway charges ahead underground before she gets off to walk the rest. Whenever she flies to Europe, she asks her neighbour to keep his copies, and when she returns she spends several weekends catching up with New York time from foot-high piles. During her lunch breaks, she clears up her desk and reads the inside pages, leaning her elbows against the edge of her desk, as Europeans do. Once, when visiting Chicago, she walked three kilometres along a street blasted by an icy, snowy wind and lined with blind apartment silos, until she found a recent copy of the New York city edition in a pro-Chinese bookstore, as if only non-local print was to be believed. By the time she leaves work, the three longitudinal folds have already become so settled that the columns willingly fold up and towards the right and left under the fingers of a single hand, like the keys of an instrument, as she needs her other hand to hold onto the strap in the crowded, rocking subway. Once, past midnight, she walked to Broadway through sweltering side streets, cautiously and with her eyes looking straight ahead, passing groups of people talking in low voices and another brawling about a drunken or unconscious woman. At this time of the night, Broadway was peopled with police, prostitutes and addicts, and she bought the earliest edition of the *New York Times*, opened it under the acetylene lamp on the newsstand roof and found the news that now held more truth than the lurid headlines in the afternoon papers that she had refused to believe the day before (that was when Mrs Enzensberger had assaulted the Vice-President in Berlin with bombs of custard powder). She keeps the folded, flapping paper under her arm until she has closed her apartment door behind her and then reads the finance reports over dinner, for work. Any time she misses the paper because she spends a day on the beach, she keeps an eye out on the subway floor and checks the rubbish bins for a copy of the day's discarded, torn or stained *New York Times,* as if that was the only way of proving the day. She relates to the *New York Times* and feels at home with it as if it was a person, and the way she feels when studying this big, grey bundle of paper is as if there was a presence, as if she was in conversation with somebody whom she listens and replies to with the politeness, the well-concealed doubt, the hidden grimaces, the forgiving smiles and any gestures that she would these days show to an aunt, a general, unrelated, imaginary aunt: her concept of an aunt. ★

Melting Pot

**From Little Italy
to Chinatown**

④

Colombian arepas meet Japanese pulled pork

Ingredients

Serves 4

For the arepas:
About 280 g (10 oz) pre-
  boiled maize flour (harina pan,
  available online or from
  specialist delis – do not
  substitute normal maize flour
  or polenta)
1 teaspoon salt
30 g (2 tablespoons) butter,
  melted
Vegetable oil for frying

For the pulled pork:
About 1 kg (2 lb 4 oz) pork
  shoulder, deboned
1 onion
1 piece ginger (about 3 cm/
  1¼ inches)
2 garlic cloves
120 g (4¼ oz) tomato ketchup
75 ml (⅓ cup) dark soy sauce
75 ml (⅓ cup) sake (Japanese
  rice wine)
1½ tablespoons rice vinegar
2 tablespoons sesame oil
2 tablespoons brown sugar
1 tablespoon dark miso paste
Chilli powder
2 tablespoons peanut oil
1 teaspoon cornflour
  (cornstarch), to taste

Also:
Sesame seeds for sprinkling

For the pulled pork, rinse the meat and pat dry. Remove any fat and tendons and cut into five even pieces. Transfer to a bowl.

Peel the onion, ginger and garlic. Finely dice the onion and mince the ginger and garlic. Combine with the ketchup, soy sauce, sake, rice vinegar, sesame oil, miso paste and sugar. Season the marinade with chilli powder. Toss the meat in the marinade and set aside for at least 4 hours for the flavours to develop.

Heat the peanut oil in a large saucepan or casserole dish. Remove the meat from the marinade, drain and fry in the hot oil until browned all over. Add the marinade and pour in 500 ml (2 cups) water. Bring the liquid to a boil. Reduce the heat, cover and braise for about 2 hours. Remove the lid and continue to cook for another 30 minutes until the meat almost falls apart. Turn the meat every now and then while it cooks. Remove the meat from the dish and set aside. Bring the marinade and meat juices to a boil and simmer for about 10 minutes to reduce. Whisk in the cornflour to bind. Pull the meat apart using two forks and add to the dish again.

For the arepas, combine the maize flour and salt in a bowl. Add about 320 ml (1¼ cups) lukewarm water and the melted butter and process everything to a smooth dough. Cover with plastic wrap and set aside to rest for 10 minutes. Meanwhile, dry-roast the sesame seeds in a pan until golden brown.

Shape the dough into eight balls. Flatten the balls into round patties about 1.5–2 cm (¾ inch) thick with your hand (about 8 cm/ 3¼ inches in diameter). If the dough is too thin for shaping patties, knead in more flour; if it is too dry or tears, add a little water. Heat the oil in a frying pan and fry the arepas in batches for about 5 minutes per side.

Halve the arepas horizontally, fill with the pulled pork and toasted sesame seeds and serve immediately.

Asian risotto with coriander pesto

For the coriander pesto, peel the garlic and ginger. Crush the garlic in a garlic press and finely grate the ginger. Rinse the herbs, shake off excess water and chop coarsely. Wash the chilli. Remove the stem, deseed and chop finely. Chop the cashew nuts and dry-roast in a pan until golden brown, stirring frequently. Set aside a small portion. Combine all of the prepared ingredients in a blender together with all except 1 tablespoon of the oil, the lime juice and honey. Add more oil to taste. Season the pesto with salt and pepper.

For the risotto, peel the shallots, garlic and ginger. Mince the shallots and garlic. Mince a third of the ginger. Cut the remaining two thirds into thick slices and set aside. Wipe the mushrooms with kitchen paper, trim and cut into bite-sized pieces, if necessary. Peel the carrots and cut into strips. This is best done using a julienne slicer. Rinse and drain the bamboo shoots.

Heat 2 tablespoons oil in a wok or frying pan. Add half of the minced shallots and all of the minced garlic and ginger and sweat for about 5 minutes. Add the mushrooms and fry everything for 4 minutes. Stir in the carrots and continue to fry for another 4 minutes. Whisk the soy sauce, fish sauce and sugar together. Pour over the mushroom mixture to deglaze and simmer briefly to reduce. Toss in the bamboo shoots and take the wok or pan off the heat.

Meanwhile, bring the vegetable stock to a boil together with the sliced ginger and kaffir lime leaves. Simmer for about 10 minutes over low heat. Remove the kaffir lime leaves and ginger. Keep the stock simmering.

Heat the remaining oil in a large saucepan. Add the remaining minced shallots and sweat briefly. Add the risotto rice and continue to sweat for a few minutes, stirring continuously. Increase the heat, deglaze the rice with the rice wine and reduce a little. Add a ladleful of hot stock and allow it to be absorbed, still stirring frequently. Once all of the liquid has been absorbed, add another ladleful of stock and continue until the rice is cooked and creamy but still al dente. This will take about 25 minutes in total. Stir in the lime juice and the mushroom mixture. Take the risotto off the heat and set aside for a few minutes to allow the flavour to develop. Serve the risotto with the coriander pesto, garnished with the remaining cashew nuts.

Ingredients

Serves 4

For the risotto:
2–3 small French shallots
2 garlic cloves
1 piece ginger (4 cm/1½ inches)
200 g (7 oz) shiitake or oyster
    mushrooms
2 carrots
100 g (3½ oz) bamboo shoots
    (from a jar)
4 tablespoons peanut oil
4 tablespoons soy sauce
½ tablespoon fish sauce
1 teaspoon brown sugar
1 litre (4 cups) vegetable stock
2 kaffir lime leaves
400 g (1¾ cups) risotto rice
100 ml (generous ⅓ cup)
    rice wine
Juice of 1 small lime

For the coriander pesto:
1 garlic clove
1 piece ginger (1.5 cm/⅝ inch)
1 bunch coriander (cilantro)
½ bunch parsley
½ small red chilli
30 g (¼ cup) cashew nuts, plus
    some extra for garnish
120 ml (½ cup) sesame oil
1–2 tablespoons freshly
squeezed lime juice
1 teaspoon honey
Salt, freshly
ground
pepper

Falafel with yoghurt dip and tomato salad

Ingredients

Serves 4 / makes about 20 falafel

For the falafel:
250 g (1¼ cup) dried chickpeas
2 French shallots
1 garlic clove
4–5 sprigs parsley
1 egg yolk
2 tablespoons breadcrumbs
¼ teaspoon baking powder
½ teaspoon each ground cumin,
   ground turmeric, chilli powder
   and sweet paprika powder
Salt, freshly ground pepper
About 1 litre (4 cups) neutral
   vegetable oil for deep-frying

For the yoghurt dip:
½ chilli
2 sprigs mint
250 g (1 cup) natural yoghurt
   (3.5% fat)
1–2 teaspoons honey
Juice of ½ small lemon
Salt, freshly ground pepper

For the tomato salad:
8 tomatoes
2 small French shallots
4–5 sprigs parsley
½ lemon
3–4 tablespoons olive oil
Salt, freshly ground pepper
1 pinch sugar

Soak the chickpeas for the falafel in plenty of cold water for at least 12 hours, changing the water several times. Drain through a strainer and rinse thoroughly. Peel and mince the shallots and garlic. Rinse the parsley, shake off excess water and coarsely chop the leaves. Transfer all of the prepared ingredients to a powerful blender and blend, then combine the mixture with the egg yolk, breadcrumbs, baking powder and spices until smooth. Season the falafel mixture well with about 1½ teaspoons salt and 2–3 pinches pepper. Refrigerate for at least 45 minutes.

Meanwhile, prepare the yoghurt dip. Wash the chilli, remove the stem, deseed and chop finely. Rinse the mint, shake off excess water and finely chop the leaves. Whisk together the yoghurt, 1 teaspoon honey, lemon juice, chilli and mint. Season with salt and pepper. Season with honey to taste. Refrigerate until serving.

For the tomato salad, remove the stem bases from the tomatoes and dice the tomatoes finely. Peel and finely dice the shallots. Rinse the parsley, shake off excess water and pick off the leaves. Wash the half lemon under hot water, pat dry and finely grate the zest. Squeeze out 1–2 tablespoons juice and combine with the olive oil. Season with salt, pepper, sugar and lemon zest. Toss the tomatoes, shallots and parsley with the dressing in a bowl.

Moisten your hands to shape the falafel mixture into walnut-sized balls; alternatively use an ice cream scoop. Heat the oil to about 170°C (325°F) in a saucepan. Dip the end of a wooden spoon or skewer into the oil. The oil is hot enough when bubbles rise immediately around the stick and the oil starts to sizzle. Deep-fry three falafel balls at a time until golden brown all over. This should only take a few minutes – keep moving the falafel gently in the oil. Drain on paper towels.

Serve the cooked falafel balls immediately with the yoghurt dip and tomato salad.

Crostini with rocket, pine nuts and sliced beef

To make a vegetarian version, simply top the crostini with a mixture of red, yellow and black tomatoes. Cut the tomatoes into small dice, marinade in a touch of olive oil and season with salt and pepper.

Take the steaks out of the refrigerator and leave to rest at room temperature for at least 30 minutes before frying. Pick through and wash the rocket. Dry-roast the pine nuts in a pan until golden brown, stirring occasionally. Combine with the rocket in a bowl. Shave the parmesan and set aside.

Preheat the oven to 220°C (425°F), using the grill (broiler) function, and line a baking tray with baking paper. Slice the ciabatta bread and arrange the slices on the tray. Drizzle the bread with a little olive oil. Transfer the tray to the preheated oven and toast the bread until crisp, about 5–8 minutes. Turn once after 3–4 minutes.

Rinse the thyme, pat dry and finely chop the leaves. Whisk the balsamic vinegar, honey and olive oil to make a dressing. Season with thyme, salt and pepper. Toss half of the dressing with the rocket and pine nut mixture.

Allow the toasted ciabatta to cool briefly. Halve the garlic clove and rub the toasted bread with the cut clove. Arrange the bread slices on a large serving platter. Top with a little rocket salad each.

Pat the steaks dry and season with salt. Heat the canola oil in a frying pan over medium to high heat. Add the steaks and sear for 1½–2½ minutes per side, depending on thickness. Season with pepper on both sides. Wrap the steaks in aluminium foil and set aside to rest for 5 minutes. Slice thinly and arrange on top of the crostini. Drizzle with the remaining dressing and serve garnished with shaved parmesan.

Ingredients

Serves 4 (as a main)

2 rump steaks (180–200 g/
   6½–7 oz each)
100 g (3½ oz) rocket (arugula)
30 g (¼ cup) pine nuts
50 g (2 oz) parmesan
1 large ciabatta loaf
   (alternatively 1 large baguette)
4 tablespoons olive oil, plus
   extra for drizzling
1 sprig thyme
1½ tablespoons balsamic
   vinegar
1 teaspoon honey
Salt, freshly ground pepper
2 garlic cloves
2 tablespoons canola oil

Thai salad with peanuts, ginger, lime and chilli

Ingredients

Serves 4

For the salad:
1 wombok (Chinese cabbage)
3 carrots
1 French shallot
100 g (3½ oz) snow peas
Salt
100 g (3½ oz) rice noodles
100 g (⅔ cup) roasted peanuts

For the dressing:
1 small red chilli
1 small piece ginger
   (about 2 cm/¾ inch)
4 tablespoons canola oil
2 tablespoons sesame oil
3 tablespoons soy sauce
   or more to taste
3 tablespoons peanut butter,
   unsweetened
Juice of 1 lime
2 tablespoons honey or to taste

Also:
A few sprigs coriander (cilantro)

Wash and trim the wombok for the salad and slice thinly. Peel the carrots and cut into thin strips. This is best done using a julienne slicer. Peel the shallot and slice into fine rings.

Wash and trim the snow peas. Slice in half diagonally and blanch in boiling salted water for 2 minutes, then refresh under cold water. Cook the rice noodles according to the instructions on the packet. Refresh under cold water and cut into manageable lengths with a knife. Chop the peanuts. Toss all salad ingredients in a large bowl, reserving a few peanuts for garnish.

For the dressing, wash the chilli. Remove the stem, deseed and chop finely. Peel and grate or mince the ginger. Combine all other ingredients in a small bowl and whisk in the chilli and ginger. Season the dressing with soy sauce and honey to taste.

Rinse the coriander, if using, shake off excess water and coarsely chop the leaves. Fold half of the dressing into the salad. Divide the salad among small bowls or plates and serve garnished with the remaining peanuts and coriander. Serve the remaining dressing on the side.

Grilled cheese sandwich, Tex-Mex style

It's definitely worth making double the quantity of the delicious tomato salsa for this dish so you can serve it as a sauce. Alternatively, serve these sandwiches with a guacamole dip: simply mash the flesh of 1 avocado with 1 garlic clove, the juice of ½ lemon and a little olive oil. Season with salt and pepper.

For the salsa, remove the stem bases from the tomatoes. Deseed the tomatoes to prevent the salsa from getting too watery, then dice finely. Rinse the coriander, shake off excess water and finely chop the leaves. Peel and halve the half onion and slice into fine rings. Toss all of the prepared ingredients with the olive oil and lime juice in a small bowl and season with sugar, chilli flakes, sea salt and pepper.

For the mayonnaise, mince the chipotle chilli (quantity to taste, depending on the desired heat) and whisk together with the remaining ingredients.

For the sandwiches, butter one side of each slice of bread. Heat a griddle pan and toast the bread slices in batches until crisp, buttered side down. Meanwhile, remove the stem bases from the tomatoes and slice.

Preheat the oven to 200°C (400°F). Place half of the bread slices on a baking tray lined with baking paper, toasted side down. Spread the tops with a little chipotle mayonnaise. Top with some salsa and a slice of tomato and cheddar each. Thinly spread the remaining bread slices with mayonnaise on the untoasted side. Place on top of the sandwiches and press on gently. Place the sandwiches in the oven to heat through and melt the cheese, about 5 minutes.

Ingredients

Serves 4

For the sandwiches:
8 slices of light
  sourdough bread
8 teaspoons butter
2 ripe tomatoes
8 large slices of cheddar cheese

For the salsa:
4 ripe roma (plum) tomatoes
2 sprigs coriander (cilantro)
½ small red onion
3 teaspoons olive oil
Juice of ½ lime
½ teaspoon brown sugar
¼ teaspoon chilli flakes
Sea salt, freshly ground black
  pepper

For the chipotle mayonnaise:
½–1 chipotle chilli
  (in adobo sauce)
125 g (½ cup) mayonnaise
2 tablespoons ketchup
Zest and juice of ½ lime

Chinese chicken wings

This recipe fuses traditional American chicken wings with spices from the Far East. The marinade made of ginger, soy sauce, peanut oil and five spice powder makes the chicken really tender and gives it incredible flavour. Serve the wings with fluffy, fragrant jasmine rice or a fresh green salad.

Ingredients

Serves 4

About 1 kg (2 lb 4 oz) chicken
  wings (tips removed)
1 piece ginger (about 3 cm/
  1¼ inches)
2 garlic cloves
4 spring onions (scallions)
2 tablespoons peanut oil
100 ml (generous ⅓ cup) dark
  soy sauce
2 tablespoons Chinese rice wine
  (Shaoxing wine)
4 tablespoons honey
1 teaspoon five spice powder
1 star anise

Use a sharp knife to halve the chicken wings at the joint, if necessary. Peel and mince the ginger and garlic. Wash, trim and finely slice the spring onions.

Heat the oil in a large wok over medium to high heat. Add the chicken and sear until golden brown, first on the skin side, then on the other side. (If you don't have a wok, we recommend using two pans and dividing the ingredients among them.) Reduce the heat. Add the ginger and garlic and sweat briefly. Deglaze the chicken wings with soy sauce and rice wine. Stir in the honey and spices. Add enough water so that the chicken is at least half covered with liquid.

Simmer the chicken wings in the sauce for about 30 minutes, uncovered, over low heat to make sure the meat is very tender and comes off the bones easily. Add a little more water if needed. Remove the star anise and serve the chicken wings in the sauce garnished with spring onions.

Shakshuka

Shakshuka is a Jewish egg dish from Northern Africa that is usually served for breakfast. It goes very well with the onion bialys from page 78. If you prefer to keep things simple, serve shakshuka with toasted flatbread or white bread instead.

Preheat the oven to 220°C (425°F), using the grill (broiler) function. Quarter the capsicums. Remove the stems, seeds and white membranes and place them on a baking tray lined with baking paper, skin side up. Grill the capsicums on the top rack until their skins turn black and blistery. This will take about 15 minutes. Immediately transfer the capsicums to a bowl, cover with plastic wrap and leave to cool. This should make it easy to remove the capsicum skins – just slide them off with your fingers. Cut the peeled capsicums into strips.

Peel the garlic and onion. Mince the garlic and slice the onion into rings. Wash the chilli. Remove the stem, deseed and chop finely. Drain the peeled tomatoes, reserving the juice. Remove the stem bases from the tomatoes and chop coarsely.

Heat the oil in a large frying pan. Add the onions and garlic and sweat for 5 minutes until translucent. Stir in the prepared capsicums and chilli and continue to fry for a few more minutes. Add the tomato paste. Continue to fry while stirring in the tomatoes, reserved tomato juice and spices. Bring everything to a boil, then reduce the heat and simmer the tomato and capsicum mixture for about 30 minutes, stirring occasionally. Season with 1–2 teaspoons sugar, salt and pepper. Remove the bay leaves.

Make four wells in the mixture. Crack the eggs, one after the other, and gently slide them into the wells. Season the eggs lightly with salt and pepper. Carefully stir some of the egg whites into the vegetable mixture without breaking the yolks. Cover the pan and allow the eggs to set in the sauce for about 15 minutes.

Meanwhile, rinse the parsley, shake off excess water and coarsely tear the leaves. Drizzle the shakshuka with a little olive oil to taste, garnish with parsley and serve immediately.

Ingredients

Serves 4

1 large yellow capsicum (pepper)
2 large red capsicums (peppers)
2 garlic cloves
2 small onions
1 small green chilli
800 g (1 lb 12 oz) peeled tomatoes (from a tin)
2 tablespoons olive oil, plus extra for drizzling
1½ tablespoons tomato paste (concentrated purée)
1 teaspoon ground cumin
1 teaspoon sweet paprika powder
½ teaspoon ground cinnamon
½ teaspoon ground coriander
¼ teaspoon ground cardamom
2 bay leaves
Sugar
Salt, freshly ground pepper
4 eggs
4 sprigs parsley

Pierogi with sauerkraut and mushroom.

Ingredients

Serves 4–6

For the dough:
About 475 g (generous 3 cups)
   plain flour, plus some extra
   for dusting
1 teaspoon salt
1 egg
30 g (2 tablespoons) butter,
   softened

For the filling:
1 small onion
200 g (7 oz) mixed mushrooms
250 g (9 oz) sauerkraut
   (from a jar)
4 sprigs parsley
1 tablespoon each canola oil
   and butter
60 g (2 oz) bacon, diced
200 g (7 oz) low-fat quark
100 g (scant ½ cup) crème
   fraîche
Salt, freshly ground pepper

For the sauce:
1 small onion
4 sprigs parsley
1½ tablespoons butter
1½ tablespoons plain
   (all-purpose) flour
250 ml (1 cup) cream
250 ml (1 cup) milk
Salt, freshly ground pepper
Freshly grated nutmeg

To make the dough, combine the flour and salt in a bowl. Make a well in the centre. Crack the egg and slide it into the well. Add the softened butter and about 150 ml (generous ½ cup) lukewarm water. Knead everything well, gradually adding another 50 ml (¼ cup) lukewarm water to make a smooth, elastic dough. Add a little more flour if the dough is too sticky or a bit more water if it seems too dry. Cover the dough and chill for about 30 minutes.

Meanwhile, peel and finely dice the onion for the filling. Wipe the mushrooms with paper towels, trim and cut into small pieces. Drain the sauerkraut well. Rinse the parsley, shake off excess water and finely chop the leaves.

Heat the oil and butter in a frying pan. Add the onion and sweat until translucent. Stir in the bacon and mushrooms and continue to fry for about 8 minutes until most of the liquid has evaporated. Combine with the sauerkraut and parsley. Transfer the quark and crème fraîche to a large bowl and toss with the cooked ingredients from the pan. Season everything generously with salt and pepper.

Dust your worktop with flour. Halve the dough and roll it out thinly, about 2–3 mm (¹⁄₁₆–⅛ inch). Use a cookie cutter or glass to cut out rounds of dough (8 cm/3¼ inches). Knead the offcuts together with the remaining dough. Place 1 heaped teaspoon of the filling onto the centre of each dough circle. Fold the dough over to make a semicircle. Use a fork to press the edges firmly together. Repeat with the remaining dough and filling.

Peel and finely dice the onion for the sauce. Rinse the parsley, pat dry and finely chop the leaves. Heat the butter in a large frying pan. Add the onion and fry for 5 minutes. Dust with the flour over low heat and briefly sweat, being careful not to allow the flour to take on colour. Stir in the cream and milk, bring everything to a boil and simmer for a few minutes until the sauce thickens. Season the mixture with salt, pepper and nutmeg and combine with the parsley.

Meanwhile, bring plenty of salted water to a boil in a large pan and cook the pierogi in 2–3 batches. Simmer each batch over medium heat for 10–12 minutes or until the pierogi rise to the top. Remove with a slotted spoon, drain and divide among plates. Serve with the sauce.

PIEROGI are a traditional Eastern European dish of filled pasta shapes that has become very popular among New Yorkers in recent years. Allow your imagination to run wild with the fillings and feel free to experiment: bacon, spinach and potatoes all make delicious alternatives.

Spicy burritos with mince, avocado and beans

Remove the stem bases from the tomatoes and dice. Wash the chilli. Remove the stem, deseed and chop finely. Peel the onion and garlic. Mince the garlic and finely dice the onion. Rinse the beans and corn and drain well.

Halve the avocados, remove the stones and transfer the avocado flesh to a bowl. Combine immediately with the lime juice and olive oil and mash finely using a fork. Season the guacamole with salt, pepper and chilli flakes.

Heat the canola oil in a frying pan over medium to high heat. Add the minced meat and sear for a few minutes until crumbly. Reduce the heat a little. Stir in the onion, garlic and chilli and sweat everything for a few minutes. Add the tomato paste and fry briefly, then deglaze the mixture with the stock. Stir in the tomatoes and simmer, uncovered, for about 10 minutes. Season generously with salt, pepper and sugar. Combine with the beans and corn and heat through briefly.

Heat a second pan and warm up the tortillas one at a time. Spread each tortilla with a quarter of the grated cheddar along the middle, making a strip about 4 cm (1½ inches) wide. Allow the cheese to melt, leaving a margin of about 3 cm (1¼ inches) on the sides. Only heat the tortillas through for about 3 minutes; otherwise they turn hard and will be difficult to roll up.

Meanwhile, wash and trim the lettuce leaves and cut into strips. Remove a hot tortilla from the pan and top the melted cheddar with a quarter of the minced meat mixture. Spread with a little guacamole and top with some lettuce strips. Fold the short edges over the filling. Fold in one of the long sides and roll up the burrito tightly towards the other long side. Repeat with the remaining tortillas. Serve the burritos immediately.

Ingredients

Serves 4 (makes 4 burritos)

2 large tomatoes
1 red chilli
1 onion
1 garlic clove
100 g (3½ oz) kidney beans
   (from a tin)
100 g (3½ oz) corn (from a tin)
2 large, ripe avocados
Juice of 1 lime
2 tablespoons olive oil
Salt, freshly ground pepper
¼ teaspoon chilli flakes
1 tablespoon canola oil
250 g (9 oz) minced beef
2 tablespoons tomato paste
   (concentrated purée)
About 100 ml (generous ⅓ cup)
   beef stock
1 pinch sugar

Also:
4 wheat tortillas
120 g (1¼ cups) grated cheddar
   cheese
4 cos lettuce leaves

Hot stir-fried noodles with prawns

If you have no fresh king prawns, simply substitute frozen ones. Another delicious alternative is to replace the prawns with pan-fried salmon fillets.

Ingredients

Serves 4

250 g (9 oz) mie noodles
  (Asian egg noodles)
2 shallots
1 garlic clove
1 small piece ginger
  (about 2 cm/¾ inch)
1 carrot
½ red chilli
120 g (4¼ oz) bamboo shoots
  (from a jar)
About 300 g (10½ oz)
  fresh king prawns (jumbo
  shrimp), peeled and deveined
5 tablespoons peanut oil
250 ml (1 cup) vegetable stock
6 tablespoons soy sauce
4 tablespoons sweet chilli sauce
2 tablespoons fish sauce
1 teaspoon brown sugar

<u>Also:</u>
4–6 tablespoons cashew nuts
1 lime
Fresh coriander (cilantro) leaves
  for garnish

Cook the noodles until just al dente according to the instructions on the packet. Strain, refresh under cold water and drain well. Coarsely chop the cashew nuts and dry-roast in a pan until golden brown.

Peel the shallots, garlic, ginger and carrot. Cut the shallots into rings and mince the garlic and ginger. Cut the carrot into fine strips, best using a julienne slicer. Wash the chilli. Remove the stem, deseed and mince. Drain the bamboo shoots well.

Rinse the prawns well under cold water and pat dry thoroughly. Heat 2 tablespoons oil in a large wok. If you don't have a wok, it is best to divide the ingredients among two frying pans. Fry the prawns for 3–4 minutes, tossing them repeatedly, until they are just cooked. Remove them from the wok and set them aside on a plate.

Heat the remaining oil in the wok. Add the shallots, garlic, ginger, carrot and chilli and stir-fry for 3 minutes. Deglaze with the stock, then add the cooked noodles and bamboo shoots. Stir in the soy, chilli and fish sauces. Simmer for 2 minutes, stirring, and season with brown sugar. Return the prawns to the wok and heat through briefly.

Juice 1 lime and stir the juice into the noodle and prawn mixture. Divide the noodles and prawns among plates and serve garnished with the toasted cashew nuts and coriander leaves.

THE
DIARY
OF A
NEW
YORK
LADY

Dorothy Parker

MONDAY. Breakfast tray about eleven; didn't want it. The champagne at the Amorys' last night was *too* revolting, but what *can* you do? You can't stay until five o'clock on just *nothing*. They had those *divine* Hungarian musicians in the green coats, and Stewie Hunter took off one of his shoes and led them with it, and it *couldn't* have been funnier. He is *the* wittiest number in the *entire* world; he *couldn't* be more perfect. Ollie Martin brought me home and we both fell asleep in the car—*too* screaming. Miss Rose came about noon to do my nails, simply covered with *the* most divine gossip. The Morrises are going to separate *any minute*, and Freddie Warren *definitely* has ulcers,

and Gertie Leonard simply *won't* let Bill Crawford out of her sight even with Jack Leonard *right there in the room*, and it's all *true* about Sheila Phillips and Babs Deering. It *couldn't* have been more thrilling. Miss Rose is *too* marvellous; I really think that a lot of times people like that are a lot more intelligent than a lot of people. Didn't notice until after she had gone that the damn fool had put that *revolting* tangerine-colored polish on my nails; *couldn't* have been more furious. Started to read a book, but too nervous. Called up and found I could get two tickets for the opening of *Run like a Rabbit* tonight for forty-eight dollars. Told them they had *the* nerve of the world, but what *can* you do? Think Joe said he was dining out, so telephoned

some *divine* numbers to get someone to go to the theatre with me, but they were all tied up. Finally got Ollie Martin. He *couldn't* have more poise, and what do *I* care if he *is* one? *Can't* decide whether to war the green crepe or the red wool. Every time I look at my fingernails, I could *spit*. *Damn* Miss Rose.

TUESDAY. Joe came barging into my room this morning at *practically nine o'clock. Couldn't* have been more furious. Started to fight, but *too* dead. Know he said he wouldn't be home to dinner. Absolutely *cold* all day; couldn't *move*. Last night *couldn't* have been more perfect. Ollie and I dined at Thirty-Eight East, absolutely *poisonous* food, and not one *living* soul that you'd be seen *dead* with, and *Run like a Rabbit* was *the* world's worst. Took Ollie up to the Barlows' party and it *couldn't* have been more attractive—*couldn't* have been more people absolutely *stinking*. They had those Hungarians in the green coats, and Stewie Hunter was leading them with a fork— everybody simply *died*. He had yards of green toilet paper hung around his neck like a lei; he *couldn't* have been in better form. Met a *really new number*, very tall, *too* marvellous, and one of those people that you can *really* talk to them. I told him sometimes I get so *nauseated* I could *yip*, and I felt I absolutely *had* to do something like write or paint. He said why didn't I write or paint. Came home alone; Ollie passed out *stiff*. Called up the new number three times today to get him to come to dinner and go with me to the opening of *Never Say Good Morning*, but first he was out and then he was all tied up with his mother. Finally got Ollie Martin. Tried to read a book, but couldn't sit still. *Can't* decide whether to wear the red lace or the pink with the feathers. Feel *too* exhausted, but what can you do? ★

Rooftop Bars

Above the New York rooftops

5

Negroni

Wash the orange under hot water. Pat dry and slice off two large strips of the zest (avoiding the bitter white skin underneath).

Place 4 ice cubes each into two tumbler glasses. Top with half each of the gin, vermouth, Campari and blood orange juice. Use a cocktail spoon to stir for about 30 seconds until everything is mixed well. Garnish the rims of the glasses with the orange zest and serve immediately.

Ingredients

Makes 2 tumbler glasses

60 ml (2 fl oz) gin
60 ml (2 fl oz) red vermouth
60 ml (2 fl oz) Campari
60 ml (¼ cup) freshly squeezed
   blood orange juice

Also:
½ orange
Ice cubes

Cosmopolitan

Wash 1 lime and pat dry. Slice off two thin slices and set aside. Juice both limes. You'll need about 200 ml (7 fl oz) juice.

Pour the vodka, cranberry and lime juices and Cointreau into a cocktail shaker, add the ice cubes and shake well.

Strain the Cosmopolitan into two cocktail glasses through a cocktail strainer. Serve garnished with a slice of lime each.

Ingredients

Makes 2 cocktail glasses

40 ml (1¼ fl oz) vodka citron
50 ml (scant ¼ cup) cranberry
   juice
20 ml (½ fl oz) Cointreau
4 ice cubes

Also:
2 large limes

Long Island Iced Tea

Ingredients

Makes 2 long drink glasses

40 ml (1¼ fl oz) gin
40 ml (1¼ fl oz) vodka
40 ml (1¼ fl oz) white rum
20 ml (½ fl oz) Triple Sec
40 ml (2 tablespoons) freshly
    squeezed orange juice
20 ml (1 tablespoon) freshly
    squeezed lemon juice
4 ice cubes

Also:
Crushed ice
Cola

Pour the gin, vodka, rum, Triple Sec, orange and lemon juices into a cocktail shaker, add the ice cubes and shake well for 10–15 seconds.

Fill the glasses about a third full with crushed ice. Pour the cocktail on top through a cocktail strainer. Fill up with cola and serve immediately.

Old Fashioned

Ingredients

Makes 2 tumbler glasses

120 ml (4 fl oz) Bourbon whiskey
4 cocktail spoons (about 20 ml/
    1 tablespoon) Angostura
    bitters
2 cocktail spoons (about 10 ml/
    ½ tablespoon) sugar syrup

Also:
1 lemon
Ice cubes

Wash the lemon under hot water. Pat dry and slice off four large strips of the zest (avoiding the bitter white skin underneath).

Divide the whiskey, Angostura bitters and sugar syrup evenly between the two tumbler glasses. Add 3 ice cubes and 1 lemon zest to each glass. Use a cocktail spoon to stir for about 30 seconds.

Top up the glasses all the way with more ice cubes and stir for another 30 seconds. Garnish the rims of the glasses with the remaining lemon zest and serve immediately.

MINI-BURGER

Ingredients

Makes about 20 mini burgers

For the buns:

40 g (3 tablespoons) butter
180 ml (¾ cup) water, lukewarm
50 ml (¼ cup) full-cream milk, lukewarm
20 g (¾ oz) fresh yeast
500 g (3⅓ cups) plain (all-purpose) flour
1 teaspoon salt
1 tablespoon honey
1 large egg (about 70 g/2½ oz)

For classic burgers:

1 kg (2 lb 4 oz) minced beef (best freshly minced)
Salt, freshly ground pepper
1 cos lettuce heart
3 tomatoes
1 French shallot
2 pickled cucumbers
Ketchup for spreading
Mustard for spreading

Also:

Flour for dusting the worktop
1 egg yolk, whisked with 1 tablespoon water
Sesame or poppy seeds for sprinkling
Butter and neutral vegetable oil for frying
Toothpicks for serving (optional)

Buns

Melt the butter for the buns and leave to cool a little. Combine the water and milk, crumble in the yeast and stir to dissolve. Combine the flour and salt in a bowl. Add the yeast mixture, cooled butter, honey and egg. Knead everything for about 6 minutes to make a smooth, pliable dough. Cover the bowl with plastic wrap and leave the dough to rise in a warm spot for about 1½ hours. Dust your worktop and hands with flour and press or roll out the dough to about 1.5 cm (⅝ inch) thick.

Preheat the oven to 200°C (400°F) and line a baking tray with baking paper. Use a cookie cutter or small glass to cut out 20 rounds from the dough (about 5 cm/2 inches). Place the rounds onto the baking tray at a little distance to each other. Brush the buns with whisked egg yolk and sprinkle with poppy seeds or sesame seeds to taste. Bake in the preheated oven for 12–15 minutes, until golden brown. If you would like a bit more colour, switch the oven to the grill (broiler) function for the last few minutes. Remove the tray from the oven and leave the buns to cool, covered with a damp paper towels to keep them nice and soft.

Prepare classic, cheese or veggie burgers or a combination of all three – in this case use a third of the quantities given.

Classic burgers

For classic burgers, season the minced meat with salt and pepper and knead well to combine. Form into 20 balls of about 50 g (2 oz) each and use your hands to flatten these into patties. Wash and trim the lettuce leaves and tear into small pieces. Remove the stem bases from the tomatoes and slice the tomatoes. Peel the shallot and cut into rings. Finely dice the pickled cucumbers.

Halve the buns horizontally and spread each half with butter. Heat a frying pan. Add the buns, cut and buttered side down, and toast for a few minutes. Wipe the pan clean and add a little oil to heat. Fry the burger patties in batches for about 2½ minutes per side, turning once. Meanwhile, spread the bun bottoms with ketchup and top with lettuce, tomato slices and shallot rings. Spread the tops with mustard. Place the patties on the prepared bottoms, sprinkle with diced pickled cucumber and top with the remaining bun halves. Skewer with toothpicks to hold everything together, if you like, and serve immediately.

MINI-BURGER

Ingredients

For cheeseburgers:

1 kg (2 lb 4 oz) mixed minced
    meat (best freshly minced)
Salt, freshly ground pepper
5 square slices of
    cheddar cheese
1 small red onion
2 pickled cucumbers
Ketchup for spreading
Mayonnaise for spreading

For veggie burgers:

2 small, slim eggplants
    (aubergines)
2 zucchini (courgettes)
4 tomatoes
2 sprigs thyme
Olive oil for drizzling
Salt, freshly ground pepper
3 large pieces of bocconcini
4 sprigs basil
Pesto rosso for spreading

Cheeseburgers

For cheeseburgers, prepare the minced meat as described on the previous page. Quarter the cheddar slices. Peel and finely dice the onion and slice the pickled cucumbers. Toast the buns as described previously. Wipe the pan clean and add a little oil to heat. Fry the burger patties in batches for about 3–4 minutes per side. Top with a slice of cheddar each once you have flipped them over. Spread the bun bottoms with ketchup and top with diced onion and pickle slices. Spread the top halves with mayonnaise. Top the prepared bottoms with the cheese patties and remaining bun halves. Insert toothpicks to hold everything together and serve immediately.

Veggie burgers

For veggie burgers, preheat the oven to 180°C (350°F) and line a baking tray with baking paper. Trim and wash the vegetables and slice thinly. Rinse the thyme, shake off excess water and finely chop the leaves. Arrange the eggplant and zucchini slices on the tray in a single layer. Brush both sides with a little olive oil, season with salt and pepper and sprinkle with thyme. Roast in the oven for about 20 minutes, turning once. If you would like a bit more colour, switch the oven to the grill (broiler) function for the last few minutes of cooking. Slice the bocconcini thinly. Rinse the basil, shake off excess water and pick off the leaves. Remove the tray from the oven. Top the eggplant and zucchini slices with sliced bocconcini, return the tray to the oven and roast for another 3 minutes.

Toast the buns in a frying pan as described previously. Spread the cut sides with pesto and a few basil leaves. Stack the bottom halves with a baked eggplant and cheese, a baked zucchini and cheese and a tomato slice each. Finish with the top bun halves, insert toothpicks to hold everything in place and serve.

Roasted chickpeas

How about a snack of roasted chickpeas instead of the good old salted peanuts? These tasty nibblies are prepared in no time and go perfectly with craft beer – how about a zesty India Pale Ale?

Ingredients

Makes about 400 g (14 oz)

1 tin chickpeas (400 g/14 oz)
1 tablespoon canola oil
1 tablespoon sweet paprika
  powder
1 teaspoon ground coriander
1 teaspoon ground turmeric

Rinse the chickpeas in a strainer and drain well.

Preheat the oven to 160°C (315°F) and line a baking tray with baking paper.

Place the chickpeas into a bowl and toss with the canola oil and spices. Spread onto the baking tray in a single layer. Roast in the preheated oven for 25–30 minutes, until golden brown. Turn once after about half the cooking time.

Remove the chickpeas from the tray, transfer to a serving bowl and leave to cool a little. Serve immediately or store in an airtight container for 2–3 days.

Deep-fried olives

Sitting high above the rooftops of New York, enjoying the evening sun and sipping on a delectable cocktail – what better way to end a day in New York! We highly recommend serving these deep-fried olives with a Negroni or another of our fabulous cocktails (pages 155–156).

Pat the olives dry thoroughly. Place the flour and breadcrumbs onto separate deep plates. Crack the eggs into another deep plate, whisk thoroughly and season with salt, pepper, paprika and garlic powder.

Turn the olives first in the flour, then drag them through the egg mixture. Allow to drain slightly, then roll in the breadcrumbs until covered with breading all over.

Add plenty of oil to a large, deep frying pan (the olives must be able to float freely) and heat to about 180°C (350°F). Dip the end of a wooden spoon or skewer into the oil. The oil is hot enough when bubbles rise immediately around the stick and the oil starts to sizzle. Deep-fry the olives in the hot oil in batches until golden brown all over. This will only take a few minutes. Avoid adding too many of the olives at once, as this will cause the oil temperature to drop too much.

Briefly drain the deep-fried olives on paper towels and serve, skewered on toothpicks if you like.

Ingredients

Makes about 100 g (3½ oz)

100 g (3½ oz) large green olives (stuffed to taste, e.g. with capsicum/pepper)
About 150 g (1 cup) plain (all-purpose) flour
About 150 g (2½ cups) breadcrumbs
2 eggs
Salt, freshly ground pepper
½ teaspoon sweet paprika powder
¼ teaspoon garlic powder

Also:
Neutral vegetable oil for frying
Toothpicks for serving (optional)

INDEX

The Team

Lars Wentrup

Lars Wentrup is a designer and illustrator. Seeing the empty pages of a book being filled with life has never lost its magic for Lars. He loves listening to good music to get into his groove and come up with his best ideas.

Lars and Lisa have run an agency for communication design in Munster since 2001. **www.nieschlag-und-wentrup.de**

Lisa Nieschlag

Lisa Nieschlag is a designer, cookbook author and food photographer with family roots in New York. Her food photography has inspired countless readers of cookery books and magazines. Baking, food styling and food photography – the kitchen is the centre of Lisa's creative and culinary world.

Lisa writes the popular food blog 'Liz & Jewels' together with Julia. **www.lizandjewels.com**

Julia Cawley

Julia Cawley lived and worked in the Big Apple as a photographer for five years until she and her family moved to Hamburg, gateway to the world. As a true cosmopolitan, she is open to the world, including the world of new recipes – provided they're vegetarian. Julia returned to the Big Apple for this book to capture the city in all of its glorious diversity. As a food blogger, Julia organises international food styling and photography workshops with Lisa. **www.juliacawley.com**

This edition published in 2018 by Murdoch Books,
an imprint of Allen & Unwin

First published in 2018 in Germany
© Verlag W. Hölker GmbH,
part of Coppenrath Verlag GmbH & Co. KG
Hafenweg 30, 48155 Munster, Germany

Murdoch Books Australia
83 Alexander Street, Crows Nest NSW 2065
murdochbooks.com.au
info@murdochbooks.com.au

Murdoch Books UK
Ormond House, 26–27 Boswell Street, London WC1N 3JZ
murdochbooks.co.uk
info@murdochbooks.co.uk

For corporate orders and custom publishing
contact our business development team at
salesenquiries@murdochbooks.com.au

Publisher: Corinne Roberts

ISBN 978 1 76052 363 3 Australia
ISBN 978 1 76063 460 5 UK

A cataloguing-in-publication entry is available from the
catalogue of the National Library of Australia at nla.gov.au
A catalogue record for this book is available from the
British Library

Printed by C&C Offset Printing Co, China

Design and typesetting:
Nieschlag + Wentrup, Büro für Gestaltung
www.nieschlag-und-wentrup.de

© **Food photography:** Lisa Nieschlag
© **NYC photography:** Julia Cawley
© **Other photography:**
Anna Haas (*portrait of Lars Wentrup*): Page 7
Tatjana Jentsch (*portrait of Lisa Nieschlag*): Page 7
Michael Cawley (*portrait of Julia Cawley*): Page 7
Lars Wentrup: Page 2

Stories:
Stevan Paul, *The Great Glander* © mairisch Verlag,
Hamburg, 2016

F. Scott Fitzgerald, *The Beautiful and Damned*, 1922.
In the public domain

Uwe Johnson, *Jahrestage. Aus dem Leben von
Gesine Cresspahl.* © Suhrkamp Verlag
Frankfurt am Main 1983. All rights with
and reserved by Suhrkamp Verlag Berlin

'From the Diary of a Lady' by Dorothy Parker 1933
Collected Stories © Penguin Random House and
Gerald Duckworth & Co Ltd. Reprinted with permission

The paper in this book is FSC® certified.
FSC® promotes environmentally responsible,
socially beneficial and economically viable
management of the world's forests.

Thanks

Many thanks, dear Julia. Your contributions to our earlier New York books have
already shown amply just how deeply familiar you are with your former home city,
and you have once again captured the perfect moments for this book in your fabulous
photos. We would also like to thank Christin for her culinary support and Sophie for
supporting the project throughout. Many thanks for Verena Lorenz for her culinary
talents and active support in the kitchen. Our wholehearted thanks also go to Anne
Neier for her assistance everywhere on set.

And our final thanks to our cooperation partners: *Botz, TineKhome, House Doctor*
and *Geliebtes Zuhause.*